Building Real Estate Riches

How to Invest in New Homes for Maximum Profit

CHRIS CONDON

McGraw-Hill

New York   Chicago San Francisco Lisbon London
Madrid Mexico City Milan New Delhi San Juan
Seoul Singapore Sydney Toronto

ISBN 0-07-143683-9

Product or brand names used in this book may be trade names or trademarks. Where we believe that there may be proprietary claims to such trade names or trademarks, the name has been used with an initial capital or it has been capitalized in the style used by the name claimant. Regardless of the capitalization used, all such names have been used in an editorial manner without any intent to convey endorsement of or other affiliation with the name claimant. Neither the author nor the publisher intends to express any judgment as to the validity or legal status of any such proprietary claims.

This publication is designed to provide accurate and authoritative information in regard to the subject matter covered. It is sold with the understanding that neither the author nor the publisher is engaged in rendering legal, accounting, or other professional service. If legal advice or other expert assistance is required, the services of a competent professional person should be sought.
—From a Declaration of Principles jointly adopted by a Committee of the American Bar Association and a Committee of Publishers

McGraw-Hill books are available at special quantity discounts to use as premiums and sales promotions, or for use in corporate training programs. For more information, please write to the Director of Special Sales, McGraw-Hill Professional, Two Penn Plaza, New York, NY 10121-2298. Or contact your local bookstore.

 This book is printed on recycled, acid-free paper containing a minimum of 50% recycled, de-inked fiber.

Library of Congress Cataloging-in-Publication Data

Condon, Chris.
     Building real estate riches : how to invest in new homes for maximum profit / by Chris Condon.—1st ed.
          p.   cm.
     ISBN 0-07-143683-9 (alk. paper)
     1. Real estate investment.   2. House buying.   I. Title.
     HD1382.5.C646   2004
     332.63'243—dc22

                                                                  2003025368

Contents

Contents

Contents

Preface

Over the years, I have built four homes for my family. Since I was working for home-building companies, it was natural to build a house for my family. I have little interest in stocks and Wall Street investments. My lack of interest resulted in poor returns in the stock market. I decided to stick to what I knew best and put most of my money into my home. My goal was to have our home completely paid for with no mortgage. The plan was to sell our home and build another one as soon as the IRS would let me.

Current capital gains laws allow you to move every two years without tax penalty. I sold our first home, built and sold another, built and sold another, and we are now in the home of our dreams with no mortgage. From 1996 to 2002 we spent 6½ years growing our equity through well-planned houses that sold for big profits, roughly one-third of the selling price each time. All of the proceeds were rolled directly into the next house each time in order to reduce the mortgaged amount. Our mortgages moved closer to zero with each home, while the homes got bigger and nicer. We also built rental investment properties using the same money-making techniques.

I watched the stock market rise and fall during this time. Our investment strategy was beating the market when the market was good. In bad times, our returns look even better. It has been an amazing journey filled with excitement and Excedrin. It took a lot of effort, but it has been worth every minute of it.

Preface

Along the way, many people asked me what we were doing and how we did it. The home-building principles that are second nature to my wife and I were completely foreign to many of our friends. Even people in the home-building industry were interested in some of the unique approaches we used. These experiences inspired me to write this book.

Acknowledgments

I would like to thank my wife and family for letting me dedicate the time required to write this book. I thank Steve Mungo for allowing me to use some company resources and drawings. Dennis Dahm, Real Estate Courses, Inc. was helpful in providing information on real estate and financing. Dawn BeVard created the illustrations. *A Field Guide to American Homes* (McAlister, 2000) was referenced for architectural style information. The American Institute of Architects provided contract information and Fred Gertz provided legal council. My wife Gina, mother Gail and friend Jon Buzzell were all very helpful during the writing process. Thank you to all for your help and a special thanks to God for making this book and all other things possible.

Introduction

Although there are many ways to make money in real estate, this book teaches a strategy that is uncommon, yet time tested and proven. Many builders build their own homes and move frequently from house to house, making big profits with each sale. Very few people outside the building industry do this because:

1. They are not aware of this practice.
2. They are not builders.
3. They don't know all of the inside information that builders know about building a profitable house.

Most people are not aware that they can make money doing this without being a builder or an industry insider.

Despite the fact that a home is the single biggest investment most people will ever make, most people will look at a new house as a HOME for their family and not as an investment opportunity. You have to live somewhere! Why not make the biggest investment of your life the most profitable as well? Over 3 million people will buy new homes this year. The buyers just keep coming. Over time, real estate prices have consistently risen because the demand is seemingly endless. After all, everyone needs a place to live. Supplying this demand can open the door to wealth. This book specifically details strategies that cut the cost of building a home while positioning you to sell that home quickly and profitably when the time comes. Cost effective design and construction in a highly desirable property turns into big profits upon sale.

Consider this simple example:

Two houses are built side by side in a community. Both are the same size and have similar rooms and features. Both are for sale at market price. The first seller will make 5 percent profit. The second seller will make 30 percent profit. What makes the second house more profitable? The 25 percent difference represents the lower cost of construction for the second home.

There are huge cost differences between similar types of homes. Profitable builders are keenly aware of the subtle differences that add up to big money, and they guard this information closely. You will learn how to save money through innovative design and thorough planning. You will also learn how to build a well-planned home without giving all of the savings to the builder. The critical last step in this process is to plan for resale during the entire process in order to maximize the number of potential buyers who want to buy YOUR home. Planning for resale now pays off when you sell.

Builders do not make a killing on every house they build. In fact, profits are surprisingly low. But when you build using this strategy, you will save what builders spend on marketing, advertising, real estate agents, model homes, salaries, trucks, office space, equipment, accountants, telephones, and trailers, as well as some construction interest. In a typical market, this can add up to over 15 percent of the price of the home! These are real expenses that builders have, but it's money that can go right into your pocket along with the builder's profit.

Rental Investments

Once you see how successful this strategy is, you may want to build a few rental properties. The strategy works equally well on rental investments. Build a good house for a lot less money, then rent it. Let the equity build, or use it to fund other investments.

Most people buy older homes when they purchase rental properties. Others look for bargains that are in bad shape and then fix them up to increase the value of the property. Some investors keep and rent the fixed-up properties, while others sell (or "flip") them. Buying distressed properties and flipping them is a widely known real estate investment technique. But why not do it with new homes? Isn't new always better than used?

You are never sure what you're getting into when you buy an older home. Their attraction is the equity you gain after fixing it up. Building a new home as a rental investment creates instant equity, and a lot of it! An added benefit of having a NEW home is that it is years away from needing expensive maintenance. Once you understand this process, it's easy to build a number of rental homes that increase your wealth in increments larger than many people make in a year!

Why don't more people do this? Builders sell new homes to rental investors all the time. They typically come to the builder looking for a discount and buy whatever is left over and not sold. Often, builders will discount a home that has a bad floor plan or a bad lot. But why invest in a leftover? Go build yourself a superstar property that everyone wants. This gives you your best chance to make money.

Get Started Today!

If you approach the construction of your new home using the principles in this book, you can build your family a great house that will:

1. Cost much less than neighboring homes
2. Appeal to a wider variety of buyers when you're ready to sell it
3. Make you much more money when you sell it than your neighbors will make when they sell theirs

Build one house for your family or build a rental empire. The choice is yours, and so is the money. Start pursuing your financial dreams today. You will see how the right knowledge and great planning can pave the way to living debt free in your personal home while you amass equity through rental investments. Whatever your goals, real estate has consistently been one of the strongest long-term investments. This book will give you the keys to a wealth-building strategy that will get you building your own real estate riches!

1

The Equity Strategy

Equity is the difference between your home's value and its cost. The most common mistake I see homeowners making today is the squandering of equity. Wealth is only achieved by saving. Debt is achieved through spending. The difference is lost on many people. Before you begin this wealth-building process, decide if you plan to keep it. When you have $100,000 equity in your house and you have a desire for a shiny new car, are you going to cash out? Millions of Americans cash out their equity through a home equity loan and spend it on clothes, vacation, and/or a new car. In order to gain wealth, you must keep it as you earn it. Don't cash out and spend it like so many do.

In my opinion, it is not a good choice to take money out of an equity position that builds wealth and put that money into a depreciable asset. What is that? A depreciable asset is a CAR, or anything else that sells for substantially less than you paid for it. Homes don't do that (typically). However, cars do it in almost every situation unless it is a rare classic car. If you know your $30,000 SUV will turn into a $10,000 used SUV, why not drive a previously owned car that someone else depreciated while your $30,000 grows in value through your real estate investments?

Plain and simple, the Equity Strategy is the pursuit of financial independence through the elimination of debt and the increasing of home equity.

Wealth is defined as *assets less liabilities*. A millionaire is one who has assets (part of which might be real estate) that are worth over $1 million more than the debt associated with those assets. The assets of most people are home equity, cash, cars, and financial investments. Typical debts are people's home mortgages, car payments, and credit card debt. Assets minus liabilities equal wealth. Another way to put it is, wealth grows if liabilities go down or assets go up. The Equity Strategy raises your home equity, lowers your mortgage, and therefore increases your wealth.

The wealth of an average successful person might look like this:

	Assets	Liabilities	Wealth
House	$200,000	$180,000	
Car	$25,000	$22,000	
Credit Card		$13,000	
Stocks	$5,000	$0	
Savings	$5,000	$0	
	$235,000 −	$215,000 =	$20,000

The wealth of a millionaire might look like this:

	Assets	Liabilities	Wealth
House	$500,000	$0	
Rental Properties	$1,500,000	$1,000,000	
Car	$45,000	$0	
Credit Card		$0	
Stocks/Bonds	$200,000	$0	
Savings	$100,000	$0	
	$2,345,000 −	$1,000,000 =	$1,345,000

Stay Diversified

If you focus on real estate as a wealth-building strategy, it is important to stay diversified along the way. Keep other forms of investments and spread your risk. Keeping a variety of properties will also limit the risk of one part of the rental market going soft.

Steps to Building Equity

1. Decide if you are a saver or a spender.
2. Decide on your short-term and long-term goals (how much real estate, how much wealth).
3. Decide if your long-term goals are more important than immediate gratification.
4. Read this book and apply the strategy to your situation.
   a. Do you want this to be something you do in addition to your full-time job?
   b. Will building personal homes and rental properties become your main income?
   c. Will the extra income replace a spouse's salary and allow one of you to stay home?
5. Make a plan to achieve your goals, and then WRITE IT DOWN!
6. Stick to the plan.
7. Build Real Estate Riches!

The Cash Flow Strategy

Wealth-building and income are two different things. The best solution for achieving both is to position yourself to build wealth while providing enough income to meet your needs. Building rental properties for well below market value allows you to have a mortgage that is below what the market rental rate is. You can skim the difference each month and create a source of income. A $1200 rent on a $1000 mortgage leaves $200 per month as a "skim." Some of that needs to be saved for maintenance and times of vacancy, but the rest is yours as income. Acquiring more properties results in more skimmed money and higher income. This can replace a full-time salary in the right conditions, or it can just be a source of extra income.

As a rental investor, your tenant pays your mortgage down every month they live there. With little effort, your debt goes down and your equity goes up every year.

If money becomes tight, it may be tempting to sell a rental property or two along the way as a source of income. Selling one would give you some working capital to maintain others, buy another, or pay some bills. If you rent a new home for a couple years, you are not selling it as a "builder." Selling as an owner is a lot less complicated because people do not look to you for service work, which they do with builders. Very few people call the last owner when their heat goes out. Many people call the builder.

An alternative to selling is to cash out some equity in one of the rental properties that has a good skim. As I said earlier, I never like to cash out equity, but it's better than selling a property if you need cash flow. If you have a rental with a mortgage payment that is much less than the rental income, you can refinance it and turn the home's equity into cash. The new mortgage payment will be higher but hopefully still below the monthly rental income. Keeping the property allows you to continue building equity as you pay down the mortgage over time.

So Where Do You Start?

How do you begin? I suggest you start with building yourself a new family home and get familiar with the strategies in the book. Figure out the process and build some relationships with lenders, builders, and an attorney. To make wise decisions, you'll have to contain your emotions, balancing what you'd like in a house with what's practical. And to grasp what's practical, learn what goes into planning and building a home. Once you get the hang of it, do it again and again until you've reached your goals.

Don't Get Emotional

One of the golden rules for making investments is to be cool, calculating, patient, and, most of all, don't let emotions enter the decision. Don't ignore your heart, but don't let it override your mind either. Letting emotions enter the decision-making process clouds judgment and often causes you to make mistakes.

I remember my father's first attempt at teaching me this lesson. When I was young, we put an ad in the paper for a Go-Cart. A guy called with what sounded like a great one. He said it was custom made in California, and had Baja tube framing, balloon tires, and a torque converter. It really moved, he said. As my dad and I drove up to the house, he said, "Chris, this guy wants $200. I don't want to pay that much, so play it cool. Act like it's nothing special so we can negotiate him down." I said, "Okay, Dad, I got it." As we walked up the driveway, I saw it displayed diagonally across the driveway. I immediately started sprinting toward the most beautiful royal blue, sleek work of art I had ever seen. I was bouncing up and down with excitement as my father "negotiated" the deal. Two hundred dollars later, we owned it. I lucked out that time. The price was fair. We sold it years later for the same $200 we paid for it. However, I have never forgotten the feeling of knowing better and losing control anyway.

I am grateful for this lesson for two reasons. First, I learned it with my dad's money. Second, I have used that experience to prevent similar mistakes while buying cars, a home, and other major purchases in my life. As hard as it is to do, my wife Gina and I try to keep emotions out of the decision-making process and base the final decision on economics. The same principle holds true with the home-building process. A home is probably the single biggest investment you will make in your life. If you ever apply this rule, it should be now! All too often people let their emotions guide their decisions when they buy or build. "I want an all brick house … with a pool … and it has got to be at least 2300 square feet because my sister has 2200 square feet." It is very difficult to keep emotions out of it. After all, you are building your HOME. It's as personal as it gets, right? The trick is to build the house you want and also have it make economic sense.

So How Do I Do That?

What features should you include in a new home? How do you go about making those decisions? There are many factors that influence why we want certain features in our new home and where we want to build it. Some of these factors include:

- Family size
- Age
- School systems
- Community preference
- Commute
- Affordability
- How long you intend to live there
- Personal taste

After asking yourself what you want in a new home, ask yourself if all those things will pay for themselves when you sell it. Will the next purchaser of this home pay me what this feature is worth? You may be asking yourself why should you care about resale. Chances are, you will only live there a few years. Unexpected changes in job, family, marriage, or other circumstances sometimes cause families to move out of a new home sooner than they planned. It is always important to build a house that will easily resell, even if you plan to live there awhile.

When building a new home, you can do one of the following things:

1. Hire a builder to build it for you.
2. Hire a manager to help with the daily management.
3. In some places, act as your own general contractor without a building license and hire the subcontractors directly.

Whether you are building or having it built, there are valuable design, construction, and marketing techniques that can make your house a profitable investment as well as a home.

When asked to provide pricing on a customer's home plans, most builders will do just that. They will price what you give them. They are not likely to engage in cost-savings discussions with you. The plans that you pick might have numerous inefficiencies that drive up the cost. The builder will tack a mark-up on top of the cost and give you their price. You could waste tens of thousands of dollars without even knowing it. As you read the rest of the book, you will learn how to look for money-saving designs and materials and to follow processes designed to get you more new home for your money.

Be Prepared to Ride It Out

As you learn the strategies and decide what your next home will look like (and cost), remember to plan for a rainy day. Real estate has generally gone up over time, but sometimes there are brief pauses in the upward movement. Your market could go soft. Interest rates could rise sharply. September 11 could happen. A war could start. Something could happen that might make it hard to sell your house.

I always plan to sell it after two years, but make sure I can afford to stay in the house for a long time. That way I'm prepared to ride the storm out if the market is a tough selling environment. This is important because with only one opportunity every two years to build another personal house (primary residence), you want each house to be as big as possible. One-third of $500,000 is much more money than one-third of $100,000. Make each transaction yield as much money as possible without putting yourself in a bad financial situation.

2

Location, Location, Location

There's a saying in the real estate business that the three most important things about a house are location, location, location. There are obviously many other considerations, but the location of a home is the first big decision. Where do you want to live? Hopefully, your answer is the same as most people in your town. What I mean is, choose a side of town or an area that is growing. Find out where the home buying public is buying and build there.

This is a principle that will echo throughout this book: Don't be different. If you buy where everyone is buying and build like everyone is building, you will have a product in the end that appeals to the masses. This may seem a little crazy, but think about it. If everyone is moving to the west side of town, go west. If one-story plans are far more popular than two stories, build a ranch. You don't want to be selling a two-story house on the east side of town when everyone wants a ranch on the west side.

The location of your home should be the hottest selling area of town. Where is that? To find out, I suggest reading the newspaper. Many papers have a section devoted to new homes. See where the big new communities are. Look for builders' advertisements. Most large builders have advertising budgets that allow frequent newspaper ads. These ads will give you great information on the housing market. Look at the maps in the ads. See if a pattern emerges. Depending on the size of the town, there may be one or several areas that have a lot of builder activity. It usually is in an area with good schools. One of the biggest factors for location is good schools. Buyers buy homes where the good schools are located. You say you don't have kids? It doesn't matter. The person buying your house probably will have kids. Schools are always important.

"Location" is more than the land that your house sits on. As a homeowner, your quality of life is greatly affected by your proximity to work, play, and all of the other places that your errands take you. Check to see if the area has good access to main arteries. Is the commute fairly typical? Consider yourself and your spouse, but also consider the "typical" home buyer's commute. Consider the area's proximity to shopping, grocery stores, movies, schools, parks, drugstores, dry cleaning, hardware stores, gas stations, day care, doctors, churches, ball fields, etc. Is it convenient to live there? Another great reason to pay attention to large builders is that they study all of this before buying land. You can bet that these questions have been answered before a multimillion-dollar investment was made to build several hundred homes in a community. Sometimes builders are wrong; but if houses are selling well in a community, the buying public agrees with the builder's research.

Long-term growth in an area usually translates to appreciation on your home. Areas grow because people want to be there. The more people come, the more gas stations, stores, doctors, and other services are required to meet the needs of those people. All these new businesses need employees. They migrate to the area as well. The cycle continues. The rule of supply and demand comes into play, and property prices rise. On top of the appreciation, you now have a home in an area that other buyers are attracted to. When you sell, this is likely to make selling your home faster and more profitable.

Sometimes a hot area of town isn't new at all. There are many established areas that continue to appreciate at a rapid pace. These areas are

Location, Location, Location

usually close to town and totally "built out"—typically, there are only a handful of lots available. Sometimes vacant lots and other "infill" pieces of property come onto the market. These may be good investments, but other means of research are necessary. Since most of the other homes are older, it is often difficult to get a feel for how desirable an area is and what type of home is preferred. I find it easier and more reliable to track new construction trends, so we will focus on the new areas of town.

Once you have decided on an area, look for your lot. You need to decide if you want to live in a community—sometimes referred to as a "subdivision"—or on an individual lot. Many communities these days have restrictions on what can be built. Check into this early in your search to make sure the "Covenants and Restrictions" match your needs. To find the right community for you, ask a few questions. Will the type of home you want to build fit in with the community? Is the size of your home consistent with the others? Does this community feel like home?

A big selling feature for many communities is an amenity center. "Amenities" include pools, jogging trails, playgrounds, tennis courts, soccer fields, etc. They are immensely popular with buyers. If you can buy a lot with access to amenities, consider it. It's probably going to cost a little more than the others, but amenities add to the quality of life in a community. You will enjoy them, and other buyers are willing to pay for them. This will help you on resale.

When deciding between a lot inside a community or outside, consider what most buyers are doing in the area. Again, go with the flow. If community living is very popular, buy in a community.

Communities are popular for many reasons:

- A sense of neighborhood. Neighbors know each other and have a sense of commonality.
- Consistency of homes. Generally, the homes are in the same price range.
- A sense of security. Even with no security measures, a community feels more secure than a road.
- Slower traffic. Since there is no through traffic, there are fewer cars and they usually travel much slower than those outside a community.

- Restrictions. Growing in popularity, Community Covenants and Restrictions (CC&Rs) provide guidelines to which all residents must comply. They vary in content, but generally govern size and style of home, yard appearance, and landscaping do's and don'ts. These are generally used to prevent residents from building or doing something obnoxious, irritating, or harmful to other residents. CC&Rs prevent your neighbor from pig farming or building a shrine to Elvis in the front yard. These would generally be frowned upon by potential buyers when you sold your home. CC&Rs protect your investment.
- Home Owners Associations (HOAs). Many communities have HOAs that govern the community business. Common areas and amenity maintenance costs may be shared by the homeowners and paid for through annual dues.

What about a waterfront lot or a golf course lot? If you're interested in a lot with a great view, you are not alone. Lots with views are very popular today. The value of these lots is often set by a licensed appraiser who thoroughly researches the market. Other times it is set by a builder or developer who asks himself, "How much can I get for this lot?" If he thinks that fairway lots on the sixth hole should get an extra $15,000 more than off-course lots, then that is the price. If sales are slow, he may cut the "lot premium" to $10,000 or less. If sales are good, he may raise them.

The point is: Be careful with this type of lot. They can gain or lose value faster than other lots. Determine if YOU think the price is right. If you think it's too high, it probably is. Before you buy, get it appraised. For a few hundred dollars, you might prevent a multithousand-dollar mistake.

3

Cheap Dirt, Dirt Cheap

The chapter title may seem redundant, but you can't say it enough. Get a good value on the lot. This is not just limited to the price you pay. Let's discuss the art of buying good dirt.

Picking a Lot

Picking a lot is one of the biggest money-saving opportunities in the construction process. Any successful building company will tell you: Buy the land well and it's downhill from there. It is remarkable to me how often builders build on lots that are steep and heavily wooded when there are flatter ones with fewer trees on the same street. Most people like trees and want a wooded lot. However, few customers understand just how expensive it can be to build on heavily wooded or steeply sloping lots. Hardly any customers are willing to pay ALL of the additional costs. The builder is the one who pays these costs out of his potential profits.

First let's deal with slope. A flat lot is cost effective in many ways. Most foundations, except basements, are cheaper on a flat lot. There is less concrete, less brick, less block, less mortar, less lumber, less siding, less scaffolding, less time, and, you guessed it, time is money. The "footprint" of a house is the outside edge of the foundation. If a lot slopes five feet downhill inside the footprint of the crawl space foundation, a builder may spend many thousands of dollars more than the same house on a flat lot. To add insult to injury, he may get complaints from the customer because there is no flat yard for the kids to play soccer. Some areas of the country are all steep hills, some are gently sloping, and some are dead flat. You do not always have a choice. When looking at a dozen lots, there will always be a BEST lot. Choose the one that slopes the least while still providing drainage.

Basements are less affected by slope. Many basements are dug down into a level lot. Others are built on a sloping lot where one side is buried and the other side has a door that opens out to grade. These are called "walk-out basements." Walk-outs are nice because they provide access and light to the basement. They are cost effective on a sloping lot. You get the benefit of habitable space where an otherwise high crawl space might have been. Buyers will pay for a walk-out basement, but they rarely want to share the expense of a seven-foot crawl space. It has no marketable value.

Trees only matter on a lot when they live. All too often trees are damaged or killed during the construction process no matter how hard we try to preserve them. They are VERY expensive to take down if they die after the house is built. They can also cause structural damage if the roots grow under the foundation. Grading the lot to provide proper drainage, especially right around the house, is difficult without destroying roots. For these reasons, I recommend removing ALL trees within 15 feet of the house. Any other tree that interferes with proper grading or drainage should be removed up front. Having said that, consider this advice when shopping for a lot: Are the trees that you like inside the footprint of the house or within the 15-foot perimeter? Consider the drainage pattern and its effect on trees. Then ask yourself how many trees are left. How many are you going to have to pay to remove? Consider these costs carefully in your decision.

The first house that I built for my family was on a lot that used to be a trash pile and burning area. There were homes going up all around this lot, but nobody bought that one. It was in a heavily wooded community with steeply sloping lots. In fact, much of the community's appeal was due to the rolling landscape and shade trees. This particular lot was dead flat without one tree. It didn't even have any weeds or vegetation, due to the trash that had recently been stockpiled and removed. I got it at a discount. (Why? Because I asked for one. Always ask.) The first nickel I spent on construction was digging the footing. Most other lots in the community would have had at least $1800 in clearing costs and additional foundation costs of about $3000. I put in a great landscaping package after I finished the house, and hardly missed the trees. The money I saved allowed me to build a bigger house than I would otherwise have been able to afford. Do the math. At about $40 per square foot, that savings buys an additional 10-by-12-foot bedroom! I love trees, but I'll take the extra bedroom every time if I have to choose. I had to make some sacrifices, but they paid off. I was very happy with the completed home, because it blended into the community. Although I got a good price on the lot, the value in this lot was not in the purchase price. It was in the lack of preparation required. Before I began construction, I had saved about $4800 that most of my neighbors' builders had to spend to get their lots ready to build on. That turned into $4800 profit when I sold it.

When shopping for a lot, do not be afraid to lowball. If you find a lot that you like but it's just out of your price range, submit a low bid that you're comfortable with. The worst that can happen is they refuse the offer. They could also accept it! You'd be amazed how often land is dumped in this business. Cash flow is the name of the game in development and building. No cash, no business. If someone needs cash, they're not going to put this information on the sign, so you have to submit an offer to find out. The best candidates for this are lots owned by builders or by individuals who have been on the market awhile. When land sits on the company's books for a long time, the accountants start getting nervous. There's a popular school of thought that counsels dumping that nonproductive land at any cost to get it off the books. You could benefit from this. Be careful, though. Ask yourself why the land has not sold yet. Make sure it's not a lemon. It could be a number of things, including inadequate marketing or incorrect pricing. Or it might be the hog farm that is upwind of it. Always walk the lot, look carefully, smell, and look at the adjacent properties. If the adjacent properties are undeveloped, see if they're zoned for residential housing.

Zoning is an important consideration when shopping for land. Get familiar with local zoning ordinances. Check the zoning not only on the lot, but on adjacent and nearby property as well. Local city or county offices can provide this information. Property value can be affected by nearby commercial property, which can be an eyesore, affect traffic, produce noise or air pollution, and generally detract from the property's appeal. You need to know if the field down the street is zoned for a funeral parlor or a used car lot. There are also several types of residential zoning. Apartment complexes and other high-density housing may not be desirable neighbors. Make sure you understand the zoning of all property that affects you.

Now Look Down

Now that you've looked all around your lot, the next direction to look is down. Not every lot has good soil on it. It may look good until you start digging. Some lots have unsuitable or bad soil. The trick to being profitable is to AVOID THOSE LOTS. There are many things that can cause soil to be unsuitable to build on. A quick way to get a good idea about the soil is to ask the builders on either side, or nearby. Did they encounter any problems? This is not foolproof. Soils can sometimes be different 10 feet away. More often than not, if the neighboring lots had good soil, so will you. If you plan to purchase a lot, I recommend having the lot tested by a geotechnical firm before you buy it. Here are some of the things to avoid:

Expansive soils. These clays swell tremendously when wet. They can destroy a foundation. Expansive soils are common in some parts of the country. Other areas have small veins of this clay that run through a small percentage of the land. They can be extremely destructive if not handled properly. Don't let me scare you. Expansive soils are fairly rare, and not all clay is expansive. The important thing is to identify it and deal with it. Sometimes, a small vein can be simply removed when the foundation is excavated. It is either replaced with good soil, gravel, or concrete. If the expansive soil is too extensive to remove, the foundation is engineered to withstand the unusual stress of the soil, and other precautionary measures are taken to avoid water problems that cause the clay to expand. In Denver, the basement floors move up and down so much that the stairs are on hinges! If you live in Denver, you may have to deal with expansive soils. If you live in an area where you can avoid lots with these soils, I highly recommend that you run screaming.

Wet lots. Extensive groundwater can lead to dozens of problems. Wet lots are usually wet before you start building. They are often in a low-lying area that collects water. When rainwater has nowhere to drain, it sits around and soaks into the ground. Wet lots may also be the result of a natural spring on the lot. Sometimes the spring is uphill, but the downhill lot holds the water. A puddle of water on a lot may *not* be a problem. Lack of surface drainage does not always lead to expensive groundwater problems. A severe water problem can usually be exposed with shallow digging with a shovel— the hole will fill up with water over a day or so. Some holes may fill up in no time, and the water will sometimes have a rotten smell or a slimy texture. Wetland plants are a great clue that a lot is wet since the vegetation may change in the wet areas. Wet lots cannot be built on without being fixed, and fixing them can be very expensive. Worse yet, you rarely know exactly what it will cost until you're halfway through the process. Again, run screaming.

Flood plains. The lot may be dry, but maybe it's in the flood plain. A flood plain is an area subject to flooding in a worse case scenario. Flood plains are established locally, usually based on a map generated by FEMA (Federal Emergency Management Agency), a federal government agency, and often based on the 100-year flood plain. Loosely translated, this is the height that water would reach in the case of a flood that was as bad as any in the last 100 years. It may even be a 500-year flood plain. Obviously, this is not a flood that's likely to happen tomorrow. Homes are built all the time in flood plain areas. Personally, I would find another lot unless there was a tremendous bargain to be had. Upon resale, you don't want any issues slowing down the sale. If you do build in a flood plain, the house needs to be above the flood elevation. This means that the first floor needs to be that high off the ground, and it varies per lot. *Have an engineer establish the* *height of the foundation!* If you do not, you may be faced with raising the house after you build it. Ponder that scenario for a second. Like I said, find another lot.

Buried debris or trash will cost you money to remove and then to replace the dirt. Debris is sometimes found in gullies on old farmland. Sometimes buried debris is left by previous land owners or the land development contractors themselves. I once had to remove $7400 worth of stumps and logs that were buried on two lots. The developer's contractor buried them and covered it over with dirt. The developer paid for the work, but I could have been left holding the bag if the relationship was sour. This is very unusual, but it does happen.

Uncompacted soils. For a number of reasons, lots are sometimes filled with dirt to raise them up. If a lot is filled with additional fill dirt, it must be done a specific way and tested to verify that it is correct. Dirt is installed in "lifts," which are layers usually six inches thick. Each layer or lift is compacted to 95 percent compaction. At less than 95 percent, the ground is not strong enough to support a house. Every building site that is filled must be tested for compaction by a testing agency (usually independent). Each lift can be tested, or sometimes compaction is tested when filling is complete. Either way, all fill dirt must be compacted to specific requirements and tested. Get copies of these reports from the seller if fill was installed. If copies cannot be provided, have the seller test the lot again and certify it. If he cannot or will not, run screaming.

Ground that will not perk. If you plan to use a septic system, the lot must "perk." This is a test to measure the rate that water soaks into the ground. If it is too slow, you will not be allowed to install a septic system. A septic system is used to filter and disperse waste material from your sewer. A "septic field" is a filter network installed in your yard to disperse the liquids into the ground. If the ground is not porous, this will not occur. To test the ground, a small hole is dug and water is placed in the hole. The rate at which water soaks into the ground (percolates) is measured by the local inspector. If it passes the perk test, the lot is said to "perk." If you have access to city or county sewer lines you don't need a septic system.

Rock. As a general rule, rock means money. If you have rock, then every time you dig—a foundation, sewer line, water line, septic system, drainage swails, sprinkler system, mailbox post—yes, I mean every time, you will be renting a hoe ram to jackhammer the rock one inch at a time. A hoe ram is a giant jackhammer on the back of a back hoe. If you build in an area prone to rock, get a soils test to see what's there. If you have no choice but to buy a lot with rock on it, then estimate the rock removal cost and double your estimate. Blasting rock with explosives is an alternative that is less frequently chosen due to tight restrictions and the obvious danger to other homes in residential areas. It is generally cheaper than a hoe ram if you have a lot of rock to remove. It might be worth looking into if other houses are far away.

Organic soils are still decomposing. They may have leaves, roots, topsoil, or other matter typically found in the top several inches of the ground. It usually has an odor as it rots. Some lots have deep areas of organic soils that will need to be removed. As organic matter decomposes, it shrinks. If you put a foundation in the ground over organic soils, voids will be created under the foundation where the organics used to be. The result will be a foundation that may settle over time.

Wetlands are critical to the ecology of many species and are often protected against development, sometimes by the government. If you're considering buying a lot with wetlands, find out what you can and cannot do to them before you buy.

Tree save areas. Some areas have restrictions on what trees can be removed. An arborist may be required to survey the lot and label trees that can and cannot be removed.

Other Considerations

Size and shape are key elements in the selection of a lot. Make sure the size of your lot is consistent with the lot sizes of other homes your size in the area. If the lot size is too small, it might cause problems when you sell the home later. If you stick to the typical lot size in the community, chances are you will not have that problem. You might think that the larger the lot, the better. This may not be true. A large lot will almost definitely cost you more than other lots. You need to check to see if you can recuperate that cost when you sell. Check if other homes with big lots are commanding a higher price. Sometimes they do and sometimes they don't. Don't pay for it if you can't get your money out of it.

Another consideration is the setback requirements. Make sure that your house will fit on the lot without encroaching into the setback areas or easements. You cannot build inside these areas on a lot. There may be areas that cannot be built in, so not all of a large lot might be usable. Be aware of the easements and setbacks.

Do you like surprises? Nobody likes them when buying land. Make sure you ask if the sewer and water tap fees are included in the price of the lot. Municipalities often pay for the cost of new sewer and water systems through "tap fees" or "impact fees" that someone has to pay before YOU hook up to THEIR sewer or water system. SURPRISE! You owe $4000. It's the type of surprise that can be avoided by having it clearly spelled out before buying the lot. Find out if these fees are paid. If they're included in the purchase price of the lot, document it in the land contract. If they're not included, find out how much they are.

If there isn't municipal sewer and water service, the lot may need a well and septic tank. Wells are drilled on your land and may vary in price. They drill until they hit water. Since that may be 100 feet or 600 feet, the costs cannot be determined up front. Septic tanks are underground sewage treatment systems. Depending on the soil type, the size of the "drain field" will vary. The drain field is a network of tubes that lets the treated waste soak into the ground. The cost of a septic system varies with the size of the drain field.

Make sure you know what utilities are available at the lot. Is there electricity, natural gas, cable TV, telephone, etc.? The developer will tell you. However, I found out the hard way one time that they are not always right. I bought a lot from a developer that had natural gas service specifically included in the contract. During construction, my heating contractor told me there was no natural gas in that community. As it turns out, he was right. Luckily, I found out before I had a gas furnace, water heater, range, and fireplace installed. I got an apology and a partial refund from the developer, but I got stuck with a propane fireplace and electric heat. I guess the moral of the story is to call and check for yourself.

When you've decided on a lot, take the time to write out all offers in a contract that includes all conditions of the sale. Make sure the contract protects your interests. For example, include contingency clauses. These spell out what happens to the contract should a specific event happen. If you do not know if the lot has good soils, for instance, you could add any or all of the following clauses:

- This Contract is contingent upon the results of a geotechnical test and report performed on subject property. If the report shows results that are unfavorable to the buyer, the Contract, at the sole discretion of the buyer, will become null and void.
- This Contract is contingent upon the results of a survey performed on subject property by the County Arborist. If the report shows results that are unfavorable to the buyer, the Contract, at the sole discretion of the buyer, will become null and void.
- This Contract is contingent upon the results of a percolation test performed on subject property by the Department of Health and Environmental Control. If the test fails, the Contract, at the sole discretion of the buyer, will become null and void.
- This Contract is contingent upon the results of a wetlands survey performed on subject property. If the report shows results that are unfavorable to the buyer, the Contract, at the sole discretion of the buyer, will become null and void.

There is no shortage of decisions to make when building a home, but spending the time up front on the lot will save you time, money, and aggravation in the end.

Before closing on the lot, have a title search performed. A title search is a thorough look at who owned the property to make sure the title is marketable. A marketable title is one that has no liens, legal rights, or claims against it. The title search is not always perfect, so title insurance is available. I always get it. The remote chance of someone laying claim to the land under my house is not one I sleep well with.

A Checklist

Here's a lot checklist form that incorporates all of the items discussed in this chapter, so you can review them at a glance. Take a few copies with you when you shop for a lot. (You can download this checklist at http://books.mcgraw-hill.com/business/download/condon.)

Lot Checklist	
Look for These Items	Check
Community:	
Is it in a growing area where people want to be?	
Are the schools good?	
Is there long-term growth potential for the area?	
What is the proximity to work? (Yours and other people's)	
What is the proximity to shopping? (Food, clothes, drugstore, dry cleaning, movies, parks, hardware stores, day care, churches, etc.)	
What is traffic like at rush hour?	
Is the architecture in the community consistent with your house plans?	
Is the community more attractive than others like it?	
Does the community have amenities? (Pool, clubhouse, trails)	
Is the adjacent and nearby property attractive?	
Is the adjacent and nearby property zoned for housing?	
Check for negative influences on the lot. (Smells, noise from airport, etc.)	
Is the property in a flood plain?	
Is the lot zoned properly?	
Are there tree save requirements? If so, are there any conflicts?	

Lot Checklist (*Continued*)	
Look for These Items	Check
Community:	
Is the size of the lot as big as 75 percent of the community?	
Is there a community association?	
Are there Covenants and Restrictions?	
What are the restrictions—particularly size and architectural?	
What are the association dues?	
Does the association have authority to deal with noncompliance?	
Soil:	
Is the soil good for construction?	
Has a soil boring been done and approval received?	
Have adjacent builders had any soil problems?	
Is there evidence of wet areas on the lot?	
Is there evidence that debris might be buried?	
Is there evidence that someone placed fill dirt on the lot? (If so, have it tested.)	
Is there evidence of solid rock on the lot?	
Are there trees on the lot? How many will survive?	
Utilities:	
Are there sewer or water tap fees required to use the municipal systems?	
Are there impact fees required, and how much are they?	
Is municipal sewer available to the lot, and does it run to the edge of the lot?	
Is municipal water available to the lot, and does it run to the edge of the lot?	
Is there natural gas available to the lot? (Is the line installed yet?)	

Lot Checklist (*Continued*)	
Look for These Items	Check
Utilities:	
Is there cable TV available to the lot? (Is the line installed yet?)	
Is the phone service installed yet?	
If you need a well, what have they been costing others in the area?	
Does the lot perk if you need a septic tank?	
Are there any easements or rights of way on the lot?	
What are the setback requirements? (Front, side, and rear)	
Is the lot wide enough to fit your plan?	
Is the lot deep enough to fit your plan?	
Will the house sit on the lot and still clear all the setbacks and easements?	
Will there be a backyard for kids to play?	
Is there privacy? (If not, is it any worse than 75 percent of the others?)	
Flat Foundation Lots:	
Is the lot flat, or as flat as can be expected?	
Does it still allow for drainage?	
Crawl Space and Basement Lots:	
Does the lot slope too much? (More than eight feet in the footprint?)	
Will the driveway be too steep?	
Will the backyard be flat or steep?	
Will the first floor be below the street? (Avoid if you can)	
Does the sewer tap invert above the basement floor? (Ask the developer)	

Lot Checklist (*Continued*)	
Look for These Items	Check
Crawl Space and Basement Lots:	
Which side is the driveway on? Will that work with the house views?	
Has the developer received ALL necessary approvals for you to move in?	
Are the sewer tap fees included in the cost of the lot?	
Are the water tap fees included in the cost of the lot?	
Are the impact fees included in the cost of the lot?	
Does the developer/owner have a clear title to the land?	
Did you ask for a discount? (Offer below asking price)	

4

A Good Foundation

There are many types of foundations available. Each has its advantages and disadvantages. Probably, the biggest deciding factor in your choice of foundations is going to be geographic location. Many parts of the country have one foundation type that is predominantly used. Other parts have several that are common. For instance, in the Northeast, most homes have basements. In the South, concrete slabs are popular. In some areas, a crawl space foundation is common. (For graphic depictions and photographs of many different kinds of foundations, go to http://books.mcgraw-hill.com/business/download/condon.)

The choice of foundation is often dependent on the topography or slope of the land. Slabs tend to be used on fairly flat lots, while crawl spaces can be used on flat lots or sloping lots. Basements can be either fully in-ground on a flat lot or a "walk-out," which is used on a sloping lot.

As a general rule, follow what other builders are doing. They probably know which foundation is most cost effective in your area. They know which type the labor force is used to. This can be very important. It may not make sense, but if the local labor force is not familiar with a construction technique, it usually costs more. Even if it should be cheaper, "different" usually means more money in construction. In addition, I find that quality suffers when something unusual is done. Again, follow what other builders are predominantly doing. They probably have a pretty good feel for the market.

Some areas are particular about foundations. You do not want to learn this lesson the hard way. I have seen new houses get old waiting to sell because the foundation was uncommon. A company I once worked for built a basement on a steeply sloping lot in a part of the country where basements were not common. A basement made perfect construction sense. It gave us the opportunity to sell an unfinished basement and recoup some of the cost of the high foundation. With a very high crawl space, you can easily spend a fortune before you get to the first floor, and customers are not willing to pay extra for it. So we built a basement. And there it sat for over a year. We discovered there was sales resistance to basements. People want what they're used to. It eventually sold, but you do not want to wait that long for a buyer when you sell yours. Again, I echo the theme—don't be different. Build a foundation type that is common in your area.

The cost of construction methods varies from market to market. However, in most places a concrete slab is the most cost effective foundation on a flat lot. There are several types of slab construction, but they are all cost effective on flat or relatively flat lots. A crawl space is generally considered the next most cost effective type of foundation. Their flexibility allows builders to follow the natural lay of the land on sloping lots. On sloping and flat lots alike, a crawl space provides for a softer floor than a slab. Some buyers will not buy a slab because it feels hard or cold. There are others who will not buy a crawl space because of the potential for spiders, snakes, mice, and water under the house. Basements often cost the most, but provide a useful purpose in return. Whether finished or not, they provide valuable usable space for living, storage, and utilities.

Let's discuss the different types of foundations.

Slabs

Monolithic (sometimes called mono) slabs. The footings and the concrete slabs are poured at the same time, or monolithically. They have an exposed concrete edge after the forms are stripped away. They are fast and very cost effective. They lose their cost effectiveness if the lot slopes more than a foot or two inside the footprint of the house.

Posttensioned slab. Generally, they're the same as a mono, but they have one very distinct difference. Many conduits are cast into the concrete slab. The conduit protects the cables inside from adhering to the concrete. After the concrete is cured, cables are pulled under great tension and secured. The strands provide additional strength to the slab. Post tensioning is expensive and usually reserved for problem soils.

Stemwall slab (raised slab). Often made from brick or block, a wall is built around the perimeter of the foundation. The inside is filled with dirt or sand. A concrete slab is poured over the compacted fill dirt.

Crawl Spaces

This type of foundation uses a masonry or concrete foundation with interior piers to support a wooden floor system. The crawl space is not habitable space. It is often used for storage of garden tools and other items that are not going to be damaged by moisture and humidity. Lots with three or more feet of slope within the footprint are good candidates for crawl spaces since a stem-wall slab can get expensive and difficult on a lot with excessive slope.

Basements

A basement is used in various types of situations. There are many parts of the country where basements are used in almost every home.

Holes are dug into a flat lot and a basement is built. Small windows and limited light usually limit the basement's use to recreation rooms and utility space. Larger windows and doors are sometimes installed with the use of "wells." Window wells are retaining walls that hold back the dirt and provide space for windows and doors. These are required if the basement is used for a sleeping room or rooms. Lots that slope from the street to the rear allow a different type of basement. The walk-out basement has a rear wall and sometimes a side wall that is aboveground. Full-size windows and doors on the rear allow for open and bright rooms. If a lot is high in the back and slopes down to the street, a basement with a front entry garage is very cost effective. Often left unfinished, basements are easily finished by homeowners at a later date. Make sure the subcontractors do not put pipes and wires in your way since it will make things much more difficult later. They usually find a way to run a maze of wire and piping below the floor joists. Trying to work around that when installing your ceiling will leave you mumbling words you didn't know you knew.

Masonry and concrete are the materials most often used for basements. Masonry is generally less expensive. Most markets lean toward the slightly more expensive poured concrete walls due to their strength. Pricing and material preference is highly localized.

The Cost Effective Choice

If a lot slopes between six to nine feet within the house footprint, a basement can be a good choice. A nine-foot crawl space is quite expensive, and you get little for your money. A basement on that same lot will cost more than a crawl space, but you now have a marketable product people will pay for. Your unfinished basement is expandable space for a growing family. If it is a walkout, there can be windows, doors, and bedroom space, as well as a rec room, craft area, or whatever you want. With a crawl space, all you have is a fabulous place to put a lawn mower.

The marriage of foundation type and lot is an important one for profitability. As you look for a lot, keep in mind the type of foundation you want. There are many ways to save money on a foundation. The best way is to buy a lot that is well-suited for the foundation type and footprint of the home. On a sloping lot, a house plan that has a large footprint can cause the foundation to be very tall on the low side of the lot. As the ground slopes down the hill, the first floor of the house remains level (Figure 4.1). The deeper the house, the higher off the ground the first floor is. High foundations are expensive. Lots can slope in the back/front direction, the right/left direction, or in both directions. The width of the house may be what is important if the lot slopes side to side. The depth is critical if the lot slopes front to back. The entire size of the foundation footprint may be important if the lot slopes in two directions. Small footprints have less of a problem with slope because the short width or depth keeps the foundation height from getting too tall. This saves money with a crawl space and slab foundations.

The deep crawl space in Figure 4.2 has 605 square feet of foundation masonry, as compared to just 300 square feet in Figure 4.3. The deep

A Good Foundation

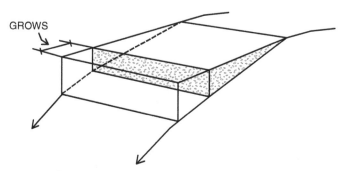

Figure 4.1   The foundation grows as the house gets deeper.

foundation in Figure 4.2 is twice as big and twice as expensive as the foundation in Figure 4.3! If you can minimize the foundation size on a sloping lot, it adds up to big savings.

Grading the lot well is the second best way to save money. On a slab or a crawl space, thousands of dollars can be saved by flattening out the lot. This is done by cutting down the high side (or high corner) of the lot. It is much cheaper to pay the grader a little more to shape the lot and cut in a drainage pattern. If you cut off the high area, you reduce the overall foundation height. If you reduce it by even a foot or two, it will translate

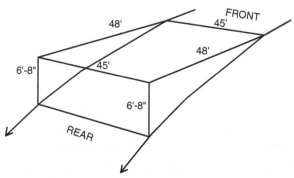

Figure 4.2   Deep foundation

Foundation Size				
	Height		Length	
Left Side:	6.5	×	48	divided by 2 = 156 SF
Right Side:	6.5	×	48	divided by 2 = 156 SF
Rear:	6.5	×	45	= 293 SF
				605 Square feet of foundation

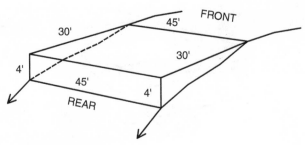

Figure 4.3   Shallow Foundation

Foundation Size

	Height		Length		
Left Side:	4	×	30	divided by 2 =	60 SF
Right Side:	4	×	30	divided by 2 =	60 SF
Rear:	4	×	45		= 180 SF
				300 Square feet of foundation	

to BIG savings. Depending on prices in your market, $1000 to $2000 a foot is the potential savings! It is well worth the effort. (For photographs, go to http://books.mcgraw-hill.com/business/download/condon.)

With a crawl space house with a siding exterior and wood-framed construction, foundation costs can be reduced through the use of "pony walls." They go by many names, most of which are equally silly, but the savings is nothing to laugh at. A pony wall is a wood-framed wall that is built aboveground but below the first floor. The masonry foundation is held down to a foot or so aboveground. A pony wall sits on the foundation and goes up to the floor level. The first floor is built right on top. Exterior siding covers the outside. The final product looks great. Instead of a high brick foundation in the rear, you have more siding. It looks quite normal since you cannot tell where the first floor is from the outside of the house. Framing and siding is much cheaper than masonry, so the more pony walls you have, the more you save. On an all brick house, a pony wall will not save money since you have to brick over it anyway.

For many builders in hilly areas, the difference between making money and not making money is determined in the foundation. Not making money, often referred to as "sport building" or "practice," can be avoided if you plan well.

5

Choosing a Style

The next major decision in the building process is choosing an architectural style for your home. There are a seemingly infinite variety of styles to choose from. However, there are some broad categories that most homes fit within. The most distinctive category is number of floors. (To view a gallery of full-color photographs of the many different kinds of architectural types, go to http://books.mcgraw-hill.com/business/download/condon.)

One-story. All rooms on one level.

Two-story. Rooms on the main level and a second level. (A one-story with a basement is usually not considered a two-story in the industry.) The upstairs rooms are usually the private rooms, and the downstairs consists of the public rooms and maybe one bedroom.

One-and-a-half-story. This term is sometimes used to describe a floor plan that has a small loft area or a small, inconspicuous second story.

Split-foyer. This is a two-story plan that has the foyer floor midway between the two main floors. The first floor is often a partial basement.

Chapter 5

Split-level. Very common a generation ago, split-levels are a combination of one- and two-story plans that are split in the middle.

Multistory. The use of three or more floors is much less common. Town homes or large custom homes sometimes use three stories. Unique lot conditions sometimes require a multistory plan to keep the footprint as small as possible without sacrificing square footage. Many attached housing units are multistory exactly because they save valuable land.

Which house type is right for you? Which one is predominant in your area? Which types are selling today? For many, this decision is an easy one. Most people seem to have a strong preference. Maybe they grew up in one type, or their last house was another type. This decision, however, should not be limited to your opinion. You need to pay attention to the market. Many markets have a wide variety of one- or two-story homes, and all sell equally well. Many areas of the country have strong trends toward one or the other. If you are going against the grain, think twice. As we discussed in Chapter 2, if everyone is buying ranches, you don't want to be selling a two-story.

"Attached" or "detached" is a choice in most markets. Detached is generally more desirable to buyers. Attached housing like town homes, duplexes, or condos is usually done to make use of a valuable location or is required to keep costs down. In some markets, everything affordable is attached, for instance, a town house community, meaning that the units are attached. They are also referred to as row houses. These are not something you should build for yourself. Lots are not typically available in attached communities. And even if one is, the coordination with another builder would be overwhelming. Either build a detached home or buy a town home.

If you pick up an architectural reference guide, you can see a vast assortment of architectural styles that were popular in American home building. Many of these styles are not built enough anymore to warrant discussion. The following are a few architectural styles that are common in modern American home construction. They are labeled in the vernacular with which most of the public is familiar. A true historian might frown on some of these generalizations, but I'm addressing you, not them.

Choosing a Style

Colonial. The term colonial generally refers to homes that resemble early colonial America. Roofs are often gabled or hipped and the mass of the house is balanced if not symmetrical.

Georgian. Georgian homes are very symmetrical. Most Georgians have single windows lined up vertically and horizontally around an ornately detailed panel door. The simple and stately design of Georgian homes make for timeless yet cost effective architecture.

Greek revival. Characterized by medium pitched roofs, round columns and front facing gables, this style is very popular. Ornate cornice and front doors give Greek revival a more formal feel. Some homes may have two or four columns that are two stories high, supporting a front porch gable.

Farmhouse. Farmhouses typically have gable end roofs, dormers, and a generous porch. Many are two stories and have clapboard siding.

French provincial. These homes are characterized by very steep roof pitches, graceful dormers and large masonry chimneys. Stucco is a common exterior finish in this style because its clean lines help keep the emphasis on the expensive roof details.

Tudor. This style includes more than the commonly known "Half Timber" detail. Typically they do have the timber and stucco detailing, but not always. Stone is another popular material on tudor style homes. Almost all versions have steep roof pitches and gable ends that face the front of the house.

Victorian. Victorian homes have ornate decoration and vibrant paint colors. Turned columns with brackets support wraparound porches. Siding often incorporates some shakes including special shapes like scallops.

Stick style. Stick style homes are Victorian, but include some unique detailing that differentiate them. The roof eaves feature exposed rafters. Gable ends often include a decorative truss, and brackets support barge rafters. Horizontal and vertical siding trim elements (sticks), provide emphasis.

Mediterranean. Styles in this category have roots from Spanish settlements and reflect adobe construction that used thick mud-brick walls with a protective covering of stucco. Modern interpretations typically include low pitched tile roofs and stucco exteriors.

Craftsman style. Craftsman homes typically have low pitched roofs and deep roof overhangs with exposed rafters. Tapered or trapezoidal columns are a common element. Decorative brackets are used at gable ends to support barge rafters.

Prairie style. Prairie style has low pitched hip roofs, deep overhanging roof eaves, and strong horizontal design elements.

Contemporary style. A contemporary or modern style may take a number of forms that do not fit into traditional design categories.

Like most aspects of building a house that will make money, choosing a style is a two part decision. First, choose the style you like best. Second, decide if the market in which you are building will welcome it. The second decision is the one that can cost you money. If you always wanted a Tudor style home, and you want to build it in a market that does not have many (or any), reconsider your choice. The lack of a particular architectural style in a market is a direct reflection of the market's lack of interest in that style. Builders will build the houses that sell. They will build anything you want. If the builders have not built or do not frequently build your style in that market, there is a reason. The buyers do not want it. It may be the home of your dreams, but it will be your home longer than you want if you can't sell it. That almost always results in a discounted sales price. It could cost you time *and* money.

Have you ever driven down the street and seen a house that just does NOT fit in. They are often referred to as "that bubble house" or "that George Jetson house." Don't be that house.

There are much less obvious trends that can affect your wallet. If 70 percent of new homes are two-story Colonials, and you want to build a one-story, you're handicapping yourself when you decide to sell. Even though 30 percent of the buyers are buying one-story homes, 70 percent of the market will not be interested in your home! Market studies are never this cut and dried. However, the trends are usually obvious if you drive the new communities and look carefully. Ask realtors or the sales agents in model homes. It is important not to look at older homes. Look at current trends.

Choosing a Style

One of the cardinal sins among architects and builders is mixing architectural styles and/or building materials. Only a handful of talented designers can pull it off. As a general rule, avoid it. Stick to one style. A classic example of this is putting Tudor style timbers and stucco on a ranch. You will not find a Tudor ranch with a low pitch roof on a hillside in medieval England! This is a pet peeve of mine. You would not have found terra-cotta tile roofs on a saltbox Colonial in 18th century Massachusetts. There are hundreds of little subtleties in architecture that make the difference between a successful design and an architectural disaster. You may not know all the subtleties, but I'm sure you've seen houses you don't like but that you can't quite put your finger on why. Something looks OFF. It's probably in the details. Conversely, the one house on the street that stands out as beautiful is likely to be architecturally accurate and proportional.

The final consideration in choosing an architectural style is the lot. The lot can rule out a few options. Consider the following:

- Is a view going to be enhanced or prevented by any style of home? For instance, a one-story house may prevent you from seeing the mountains or water that you paid to be near. Second stories typically afford better views. Maybe a two-story would give you a view you would rather not have. Sometimes no view is a good view.
- Is a style that only looks good with a one-story home going to cause lot size problems? A one-story home covers more of the lot than a two-story. With small- and medium-size lots this could cause a small or awkward-shaped backyard. If the lot slopes, a one-story house style will increase your foundation costs.
- High land prices tend to mean smaller lots. In this case, building up is cheaper than building out.

Weigh your options to make sure an architectural style does not prevent you from saving the most money possible.

6

Size Matters

What makes a good plan good? What makes a bad plan bad? Think about a friend or neighbor who has a house you like. What do you like about it? Think hard about what makes it attractive to you. I bet it wasn't the square footage. It may be the kitchen, the bathrooms, the entrance, the outside, the bedrooms, the big "feel" of the place, or the vaulted ceilings. It may be all of these things, but none of these features are attractive solely due to their size. It takes style, interest, proportion, spatial relationship, flow, and many other design principles to make a home great. If you notice, size is not on the list.

Is there a size house that's too small for you? If you think you know how big your house needs to be, I have a challenge for you. Walk the furnished model homes of as many builders as you can. Guess the size AFTER you walk through it. See if you're right. You will find that most builders build their best houses as model homes. "Best" is defined by number of sales and profitability. The houses that sell well usually "live big." They feel bigger than they are. That's why models are a good place to demonstrate this lesson. Try it and see. It is also a good opportunity to determine the floor plans and the features you like.

There's nothing quite as confusing as sitting on the couch after a long day of model shopping and trying to remember where you saw that house with the nice library. Where was that again? I have overcome my memory problems by bringing along a camera. If I like something, I take a picture. I keep a file of pictures from building magazines and photographs of features that I liked. I use this file when I work on floor plans.

Don't fall into the ego trap. The Joneses don't pay your mortgage, so don't try to keep up with the Joneses. Build a house that is sized for you, priced for you, and designed for you. I would much rather have pride in my financial security than pride in a house I can't afford.

The size of your home also needs to be compared to others in the area, especially in your community. As a general rule, you do not want to be the biggest or the smallest in the neighborhood. I like to be in the upper 25 percent for size. There are many reasons for this. Most are based on construction budgeting experience. There are also sales and appraisal issues that support this tactic.

First, let's review the budget issues. Imagine you're a builder opening a community with six different floor plans and a wide variety of exteriors available on those floor plans. You are targeting buyers just like yourself. The plans vary from 2000 to 2500 square feet (sf). All have four bedrooms. The pricing structure is as follows:

Plan 1	Plan 2	Plan 3	Plan 4	Plan 5	Plan 6
2000 sf	2050 sf	2130 sf	2250 sf	2300 sf	2500 sf
$70/sf	$69/sf	$66/sf	$65/sf	$64/sf	$62/sf

All six homes have kitchens and 2½ baths. Kitchens and baths are the expensive rooms. The major difference between the 2000 sf and the 2500 sf house is the size of the bedrooms, living room, family room, and foyer. These rooms are generally four walls, ceiling, and floor. In other words, they are significantly cheaper to enlarge than a bathroom or kitchen.

Size Matters

Kitchens and baths have cabinets, tubs, ceramic, marble tops, plumbing fixtures, shower doors, towel bars, toilet paper holders, sinks, medicine cabinets, etc. Most bedrooms, living rooms, and family rooms will have a door, a light, and four walls. The only difference between a small bedroom and a larger bedroom is floor and ceiling. It is inexpensive square footage. Look at the price per square foot for each of the houses above. Do you notice a trend? The price per square foot goes down as the square footage goes up. This is due to the addition of the inexpensive square footage.

If you get a better value per square foot on the bigger homes in a community, why not build the biggest? Well, it's human nature to live among your own kind. The people who can afford to buy the biggest home in the community can also afford the middle-size home in a more expensive community down the street. Since they want their neighbors to be like themselves and the neighbors' homes to be like theirs, they are likely to buy in that neighborhood. This means you have fewer prospective buyers when you go to sell your home. Why shouldn't you be the smallest home in the community? For largely the same reason. When you sell your home, you want as many potential buyers to see your home as possible. When your home is the smallest in a community, your potential buyer may be looking in a different community with a wider selection of homes his size.

Having reviewed a few of the reasons, you can see why being in the upper 25 percent of home size will get you a value per square foot without limiting the number of resale buyers your home appeals to.

7

Pick a Plan

After all your homework, you've decided where you want to live and picked the style of house you'd like to build. Now it's time to pick a plan. Even after limiting your selection to a specific type of home, there are thousands of possible choices out there. You can look at that as a positive or a negative.

Some people want to design their own home. Others hire an architect to custom design it. Still others choose a mail order plan package. A builder may provide his own floor plans to choose from. There are many ways to get a good set of drawings for your house, but you will definitely need a GOOD set of drawings. There is nothing more costly than an incomplete or incorrect set of drawings.

There is one constant in the building process: Decisions will be made. The question is: Who will make them? If the plans do not show how to do something, the workers on the job will figure something out. They may or may not tell you what they did. In either case, it's not likely to be cost effective, and they will probably cut your most expensive lumber in half to get the piece they need. If you aren't paying attention, you may discover what they did when you fail your inspection, which is not fun and not cheap. It is never cheaper to rework than to prepare ahead of time.

When you start with a well-planned house and a complete set of "working drawings," all of the details have been thought out. Each connection has been planned and drawn. All of the dimensions add up. The building codes have been considered and adhered to. All materials have been identified and sized accordingly. A "window and door schedule" has been drawn identifying all window and door opening sizes. Every aspect of the finishes has been anticipated to prevent conflicts with cabinets, stairs, trusses, tubs, and doors. Your windows meet local egress requirements (big enough for you to get out in a fire). Your stairs meet the riser requirements. The hallway is wide enough. The door to your laundry is large enough to get a washing machine through.

I've seen houses built from plans that are little more than a pencil sketch on a napkin. After considerable cost and headache, the house got built. The costs can be measured in labor costs to rework mistakes, the material required to make those corrections, and in time. Time is money. (Interest payments on the loan, opportunity costs, the rent or mortgage on your current residence, and so on.) A smooth and quick construction process is essential, and it's only possible with planning. A few sayings come to mind: "Prior proper planning prevents poor performance," and, "Plan the work and work the plan."

Imagine a crew of seven carpenters standing there staring at you while you look at an incomplete set of plans that doesn't show how the roof fits together in a tough spot. You can't figure it out, and the draftsman who drew the plans is not available. How long will the crew wait for an answer? Who pays for them to stand around? Hasty field decisions are much more likely to be wrong. What is my point? *You never save time or money when you fail to spend the time and money on good plans.*

Good plans do not have to be custom drawn by an architect. This is a very good and very expensive option, but it's not always necessary. If you want a home designed around your needs, or have some unusual constraints with your lot, the process of having a home designed just for you can be very satisfying. The price tag attached to this service is more than many people want to pay.

Off-the-Shelf Plans

A great alternative to custom designing your home is to choose a design off the shelf. Many architectural firms have published plans and sell them to the public. They are FAR more economical for several reasons. The obvious reason is that the plans are already drawn. When they sell the plans for a house they have already drawn, it's easy money. There's a dizzying variety available. Bookstores, home improvement centers, and magazine shops across the country have dozens of magazines boasting hundreds of floor plans. I look at them all the time. I think that 90 percent of the people in the world could find their dream home in one of these books. If you can't find one you like, look in other magazines or on the Web. Unless you plan to build a house over 3500 square feet, or you have uncommon taste in homes or unusual room size requirements, you'll find the exact house you want. Plan books tend to focus on homes of 1000 to 3500 square feet. There are many plans that are over 3500 square feet, but the selection is much more limited.

If you have uncommon taste in homes or unusual room size requirements, however, you might reconsider your choice of homes. The marketing companies and architects are selling the plans that people are buying. If you want to build a home that is not like ANY of the THOUSANDS of plans on the market, this says something about the house you plan to build. If you're truly building your home as an investment, don't be that different.

Another benefit to using off-the-shelf plans is that most of the mistakes have been found. I've never seen a set of plans that were 100 percent right the first time we built the house. There are always improvements to be made. Often there are just plain mistakes in them. The first time you build it, you find the problems. If you purchase a stock set of plans, you skip this process. Someone else was the guinea pig, and you get the benefit of that experience.

The down side to off-the-shelf plans is the lack of flexibility. There's not much opportunity to customize the plans. In fact, you need to find a set of plans that does not require any moving of walls or changing dimensions. It's easy to alter door sizes and window locations, but stay away from other major changes unless the company can make the changes on the plans for you. There are several companies that will make custom alterations to their plans for an extra fee.

Many localities will let you draw your own plans as long as they meet code. Some review the plans before you build. Some review the house during the inspection process. And some places do neither. Still others will only allow plans to be drawn by a registered architect. There are many reasons that I do not advocate drawing your own plans. First, even some of the people who draw plans for a living are not qualified to design a house. This might seem a little harsh, but it's true. To design a house you need to know design, building codes, material costs, labor costs, construction techniques, building practices, material availability, and last but not least, drafting. There are all kinds of people out there who can do some of these things, and there are a frightening number who ONLY know drafting.

When someone designs their own home, they are likely to make mistakes that will hurt them. It may be something small or it may be huge, but there's little doubt that mistakes will happen. You may get a draftsman to draw the plans you designed, but that does not relieve you of liability or decrease your exposure to costs. Whose fault is it when the building inspector fails your house because the stair landing is not big enough and it can't be fixed without moving the kitchen? The draftsman drew what you gave him. How much money did you save now? It's just not worth it. The biggest reason I don't advocate designing your own is that you're not a professional. If you are reading this book, you want to make money on your home when you sell. You need a floor plan with a WOW EFFECT! This is harder than it looks. I am a firm believer in leaving it up to the experts.

Determine Your Needs

No matter where you get your plans, you need to follow the same procedure to determine your needs. First, make a wish list. Include on this list all of the things you MUST have in the home. Think hard about what goes on this list and why you put it there. For instance, do you really need four bedrooms, or will three bedrooms and an office suffice? If an office will work, your list might look like this:

Two-car garage

Master bedroom downstairs

John's bedroom

Sally's bedroom

Office area

Kitchen

Separate dinette

Dining room

Two full baths

½ bath downstairs

Foyer

Covered front porch

Then add the things you would LIKE to the list of things you MUST HAVE:

Living room

Garage storage

Walk-in closets

Two-story foyer

Prioritize your requirements. This exercise will help you determine what is important to you. As you look for a plan, use these criteria to weed out the plans that will not work and to zero in on those that will.

One word of caution: Some room sizes can be deceptive on paper. Measure rooms in your current house or apartment to get a feel for the size room that you need. Drawing furniture on the floor plan helps. Make sure everything fits. Figure out where your TV is going. Where will the beds go? Think all of this through.

When you find a plan you like, try to see something similar in real life. Even if you do not see your exact plan, walking through a home of similar size and shape will give you a good feel for yours. You can look at model homes for builders, homes under construction, or friends' homes.

This is not always easy. But try to find something similar. It could prevent disappointment later.

After you've settled on a plan, it's time to think through all of the little details. It's easy to erase something on paper, and very costly to make changes during construction. Consider some of the following:

List of Details

1. Do all of the doors open without hitting each other or something else? Do they interfere with traffic patterns?
2. Do the window locations offer views? For example, can you see outside from the family room couch? Is there privacy where needed?
3. Do the windows have tempered glass where code requires? (Tempered glass won't shatter and cut you.)
4. Are the windows sized properly for local egress codes?
5. Are the light switches conveniently located?
6. Can you turn off the light at the top of the stairs without walking down? (We take these things for granted, but they get missed all the time.)
7. Is the lighting shown completely and correctly? Look at task lighting for cooking or other special needs. Look at accent lighting for artwork or a fireplace. Look at security lighting for outside. Check the dimensions for your dining room chandelier location. Do the bedrooms need overhead lights or switch plugs (an outlet in the wall controlled by a switch)?
8. Are there details drawn for:
   a. Stairs.
   b. Railings (and how they connect to the floor and stairs).
   c. Any blocking in the walls for cabinets, bath accessories, or grab bars.
   d. Attic walkways, if required.
   e. Roof ventilation methods. If ridge vent, how far should the plywood be cut back?
   f. Soffit/fascia detail (eave detail).
   g. Fireplace (both the fireplace itself and the mantel).
   h. Foundation construction.

   i. Kitchen and bath elevations (drawings). Show cabinet sizes and dimensions for coordination purposes.

   j. Kitchen or family room pass-through openings. Show counter overhang if applicable.

   k. Chases (openings) for ductwork to travel between floors.

   l. Skylights.

   m. Dormers.

9. Are all floor finishes shown on the plan or on a separate finish schedule? This affects how the framer builds stairs and sets doors. The flooring contractor needs this information too.

10. Is the attic access location shown? Are there pull-down stairs? How are they insulated?

11. Is the HVAC (heating ventilation and air-conditioning) location shown? If there is an outside unit, show that too. Show ceiling and floor register location as well as return air locations. Check for furniture conflicts.

12. Are ceiling heights and finishes clearly shown?

13. Are there framing drawings that show floor and ceiling joist locations, header sizes, roof rafter sizes and locations? This will save you money if it is CLEARLY defined. There cannot be too much detail here. Dimensions and notes are required.

14. Are the smoke detectors shown?

15. Are fire-sprinkler head locations shown (if applicable)?

16. Are all telephone outlets located? Is there a place for your telephone and answering machine there?

17. Is there an outlet for your answering machine?

18. Are all of the cable TV outlets located? Will the TV fit there? Is it easy to see from couches and chairs?

19. If you want a home security system, have you located the keypads and main panel?

20. If you want an intercom system, have you located the main control unit and all of the speakers?

21. Do you have any special computer wiring needs?

22. Do you want to wire for your stereo system inside the walls?

23. If you want a central vacuum system, have you located the main control unit and all of the outlets?

Chapter 7

24. Are the trim details shown for the windows, doors, base molding, crown molding, chair railing?

Your plans are not likely to show all of this correctly. Some of this is personal preference and could not possibly be anticipated by the designer. Do not be afraid to redline a set of plans. To "redline" means to draw corrections on the plans with a red pen. This is easy to do with TV, phone, or light locations. The redlines can be easily understood, and it costs nothing to do. If you're missing some of the other architectural details, I suggest getting them drawn and added. You can always staple them to the plans.

Getting details is not always difficult. A "typical" detail is all that's needed on many items like soffit, foundation, skylights, dormers, window trim, and other repetitive features. A copy of another plan's detail is sufficient. A photograph might also work if it is clear. Most contractors can look at a picture and figure it out if it's a fairly common detail. A local draftsman or architect can draw any other required details relatively inexpensively. It's worth the money to avoid the guesswork later.

8

How Nice Is Too Nice?

If you put a $2000 stereo system in a 1978 Gremlin, is that a wise investment? The same thing happens in new home construction all the time. The fact that the driver of the Gremlin really likes music doesn't make his decision any smarter. Nor does putting thousands of dollars in upgraded features in a home always make sense either. The fact that you really like granite countertops does not mean it's a good investment.

There's a principle I use in my business and in the homes that I built for myself. It's based on the belief that certain features of a home sell it, and other features will not kill the deal. Let me clarify. You're shopping for a house and look at a beautiful plan with a great kitchen, huge bathrooms, a deck, and lots of windows with great views. It's a real eye catcher. After you have fallen in love with the home, you realize that it has hollow core doors and single hung windows. You prefer solid doors and double hung windows. Do you walk away and keep looking for another home? Maybe. Most of the time these small issues go away if the house is attractive AND a good value.

Chapter 8

This chapter will focus on making your home a good value through careful selection of the features and upgrades in your home. You'll be able to save money on things that are generally less important to most home buyers. You can make money by spending money where it counts and saving every possible dollar where it will not be missed. This translates to cash in your pocket when you go to sell the home. Your home will be priced comparable to the surrounding homes, but yours will cost less to build. YOU KEEP THE DIFFERENCE! The trick is to select the items in the house that "will not kill the deal," and save money on them. These are the items that may not be top of the line or may not be as costly as similar items in neighbors' homes. However, they are items that would not prevent your average buyer from buying the home anyway.

In Chapter 15 we will discuss in detail a wide variety of cost-saving ideas. There are many opportunities to save money when designing and building a home. Many are never noticed. In the next chapter we'll talk about how homes are appraised by the real estate community. Learning the appraisal process helps explain what people are willing to pay for. This will shed some light on how to go about selecting the specification level, or "spec level," of your home. Spec level is how builders refer to the type of features and upgrades in a home. An example would be all brick, hardwood floors throughout, crown molding in every room, six panel doors, etc.

How nice is too nice? Let's look at a specific example. A person is building a home in a community whose houses are a fairly consistent size and type. There are likely to be exceptions to every generalization, but most of the houses have similar specification levels. In this scenario, the homes are two stories, 3 bedroom, 2½ baths, two-by-four-inch exterior wall framing, hardwood in the public rooms, ceramic tile bathroom floors, six panel doors, chair railing in the dining room, crown molding in the foyer, vinyl siding exteriors, sod in the front yard, seed on the side and rear yards, a small deck, and a concrete driveway. Our person in this example plans to build in similar fashion, with a few changes to suit his personal tastes. He likes brick. His house will have an all brick exterior and a driveway made of brick pavers (flat bricks). He also likes nice landscaping. He plans to have an extensive landscaping plan installed that costs almost $6000 more than his neighbors. The landscaping plan includes a number of trees, sod on the whole yard, extensive foundation plants and planting beds. Being from a colder climate, our buyer chose to make his exterior walls two-by-six inches, with more insulation. This is uncommon for the area, but it's what he wants. Has this person designed a house that is too nice for its surroundings? Will he be able to recoup his money on resale?

Is It a Good Investment?

Based on the above individual's taste, there's little doubt that he'll enjoy that house tremendously. It will be a standout in the community. The question he needs to answer is: "Is it a good investment?"

The answer is not cast in stone. You never know what the real estate market will do. Prices could rise, and a buyer might come along with similar tastes and buy the house for the right price. I recommend planning for a less optimistic scenario. Plan for poor resale conditions and be pleasantly surprised if conditions are good. In a poor resale market, other homes of comparable square footage and features are going to be priced substantially less. This house will attract a lot of interest, but will people be willing to spend tens of thousands more on it? If they can spend that kind of money, will they choose a larger house down the street with siding, two-by-four-inch walls, and sod in the front yard only?

So, back to our question: Is this a good investment? I say no. The majority of the buying public will typically like this house but will buy another one. In a typical market, you would probably recoup no money for the two-by-six-inch walls because there is little perceived value in a market that uses two-by-four-inch exterior walls. The brick house will sell for more money than the neighbor's siding house, but it probably will not be enough to make the decision a good one. Nor is it likely that you'd get your money out of the $6000 in extra landscaping. Extra landscaping is a good thing, but don't go crazy.

The profitable way to select options in a house is to limit your choices to those options that will sell for more than they cost.

We'll discuss how to figure this out in the next chapter. For now, we'll assume that we know what options sell for. If the person buying your house is willing to pay $5000 more for your house because it has a fire-place, the decision to install a fireplace was a good one. Let's do the math:

Cost of fireplace: $3400

Value to buyer: $5000

_____

Profit: *$1600, which is a 47 percent profit margin*

If the person buying your house is willing to pay $2000 more for your house because it has cherry hardwood floors throughout the first floor, the decision to install it was NOT a good one:

Cost of cherry floor upgrade: $7000

Value to buyer: $2000

_____

Profit   *–$5000, which loses everything*
you made on the fireplace
and $3400 more

I have learned this lesson over and over again working for builders. When a builder builds a house for a customer, any option selected by the customer is profitable for the builder because he just adds his profit to the cost of the option selected. It does not matter if they want six fireplaces, a 3000 square foot deck, and Italian marble on the entire first floor. Every option selected raises the profit margin. Everybody is happy until their loan is not approved or they lose their job or cancel the contract for some other reason. When the house is put on the market, it will only command a price that the public is willing to pay. I can assure you, this house would not be profitable. The builder would take a beating and may even lose money. The buying public will rarely value the excessive options at their worth.

This example is exaggerated to make the point, but it's a real problem. The same problem awaits you when you choose your options. You can avoid it by not "overbuilding." Do not choose options that are extravagant or unusual in the community. Stick close to what everyone else is selecting. There are plenty of inexpensive ways to add a WOW factor to your home. Chapter 12 touches on a few decorator ideas that I like to use. These are low risk because they do not cost a lot of money. Marble and other high-priced options are much riskier if they are unusual in the community. Consider the logic behind this. If there are 50 homes in your community and you are the only house with a certain option, then the statistics speak pretty clearly: 98 percent of the homes do not have it, and only 2 percent do; 100 percent of the people, other than you, do not have it. Get the picture? The other 49 people represent the buying public. When they buy a home, they're saying what they want in a home. More important, they're saying what they are willing to pay for. Listen to them.

Select the popular options and features you want, and then choose the ones on that list that cost less than the public is willing to pay.

9

Will It Appraise?

To fully understand the market value of options and features in your home, you must first understand the appraisal process and how it affects you. A "Real Estate Appraisal" is a report that estimates the value of a piece of real estate. Appraisals are performed on lots, houses, and commercial and industrial real estate by professionals known, of course, as "appraisers." These professionals are trained and licensed and have completed an apprenticeship under a licensed appraiser.

An appraiser will review comparable properties in the area and make the appropriate adjustments to get an "apples-to-apples" comparison. Using one of several methods, they make an educated estimation of the subject property AT THAT POINT IN TIME. As the market changes, so does the price of your home. Since very few houses are exactly the same, appraisers are skilled at estimating what the buying public is willing to spend for property, houses, and the upgrade options within them.

We will look at one appraisal method called the "Sales Comparison Approach." Comparable properties that have been recently sold are researched and compared to the subject property to determine its market value. The sales price of the comparable properties ("comps") is determined. Then the appraiser adds or subtracts money for differences in the properties until a dollar amount is reached that creates an apples-to-apples comparison.

What follows is a highly simplified but actual example. I will explain each adjustment below.

	Comparable 1	Comparable 2
Sales price	$189,050	$187,500
Quality of construction	−$1000	−$1000
Gross living area	−$4000	
Unfinished and basement	+$4500	+$4500
Garage	+$1500	+$1500
Porch/patio/deck	−$1500	−$3500
Upgrades	+$2500	+$2500
Total	$191,050	$191,500

The subject property is worth about $191,500. The adjustments allowed for the differences between each comp and the subject. For instance:

Quality of construction: Comp 1 and Comp 2 had some brick on the front of the house. Subject property was all vinyl siding. The comps were adjusted DOWN $1000 because they were nicer than the subject.

Gross living area: Comp 1 was bigger, so it was adjusted down $4000. Comp 2 was the same size, so no adjustment was necessary.

Unfinished and basement: The subject had an unfinished "bonus room." Comps 1 and 2 did not, so they were adjusted up $4500.

Garage: Subject had a side entry garage. Comps 1 and 2 did not, so they were adjusted up $1500.

Porch/patio/deck: Subject had no deck. Comp 1 had a deck. Comp 2 had a screen porch. The comps were adjusted down to get them equal to the subject property.

Will It Appraise?

Upgrades: The subject had nicer upgrades than the comps, so the comps were adjusted up $2500 to make up for the difference.

So, do you understand? Don't worry, there won't be a test. In fact, you don't really need to understand anything but this basic principle: *Appraisers put a price tag on features in your home based on what people will pay for them.* All of the adjustments are those price tags. I brought you through that exercise because I will refer to it in this chapter as a real example.

According to this appraiser, the market is willing to pay the following prices on these features:

Partial brick front:	*$1000*
Unfinished bonus room:	*$4500*
Side entry garage:	*$1500*
Deck:	*$1500*
Screen porch:	*$3500*
Upgrades:	*$2500*

Keep in mind that these prices apply only to this area at this point in time. Things change. However, we can still learn a lot. The costs for these features are roughly as follows:

	Appraisal $	Builder Cost
Partial brick front	$1000	$1450
Unfinished bonus room	$4500	$3000
Side entry garage	$1500	$1100
Deck	$1500	$1200
Screen porch	$3500	$6000
Upgrades	$2500	$1000

Look closely and you can see that several features were not good investments in this community. Brick accents and screen porches cost much more than they appraise for. The buying public is not willing to pay what they cost. You might avoid including these things in a home if you know this up front. Conversely, the unfinished bonus room, side entry garage, deck, and custom upgrade "designer touches" are money-makers. There is $3700 potential profit in those features.

	Appraisal $	Builder Cost	Profit
Partial brick front	$1000	$1450	−$450
Unfinished bonus room	$4500	$3000	+$1500
Side entry garage	$1500	$1100	+$400
Deck	$1500	$1200	+$300
Screen porch	$3500	$6000	−$2500
Upgrades	$2500	$1000	+$1500

Adjustment pricing varies quite a bit. Speak to an appraiser about your specific house and location. The numbers are certainly going to be different. Do not assume, for instance, that a screen porch is never a good idea. They may be the biggest money-maker in your area. You need to find out the needs and wants of the buying public in your market, and specifically in your price range. Speaking with an appraiser is a good start. I would approach one and be willing to pay them for their time. Simply ask them: "What options in my price range have a strong market appeal and strong value?" They may also know which ones cost less than the market value, but they really do not track that. Still, it can't hurt to ask. The adjustments they make are largely their gut feeling, so don't expect a price sheet.

Having your plans appraised before you build is a good idea. It is often required to get construction financing. By the time you get financing, you no doubt will have put a lot of time and effort into selecting plans, finishes, and features. It's sometimes worth getting a preliminary appraisal to see if you're headed in the right direction. You may not have a good idea what the house will sell for. An appraisal will give you actual figures to review, with real comparisons and current adjustment values on the features you're likely to choose. For the comfort level you get, it is $300 well spent. By the way, though it's only preliminary to you, to an appraiser it is a serious and, more important, full-price undertaking. He or she may cut you a break on the second one if it takes place soon afterward, but don't count on it.

10

Am I Normal?

We've talked about how to select a location for your home, a style for your home, the right size for your home, and the specification level. It's easy for me to tell you to follow market trends and make decisions that follow the principles in this book. It's much more difficult for you to follow the advice. In fact, it's sometimes difficult for me to follow my own advice. What you want to do and what you should do are not always the same.

My wife and I have broken some of our own rules in designing our houses. However, we did so knowing full well what the risks were. We put a few features in the house that may not make us money. For example, we love stucco accents around windows and doors on a brick home. In our market, they are very expensive. We spent money on stucco accents knowing that we probably would not recoup that money on resale. Why did we do that? We REALLY wanted them. We knew better, and did it anyway. It dramatically improved the curb appeal of the house. If we were going to break a rule, we figured we would do it on something that would bring potential buyers through the front door. They may not buy the house for a price that would recoup the cost of the stucco, but at least it would create interest in the home. When buyers fall in love with a home, they may pay a few thousand more than they should. The stucco provided enough WOW factor that we decided to indulge ourselves.

The key consideration in this decision was the belief that our tastes were shared by the majority of the buying public. We thought most people would agree that the stucco was beautiful. The title of this chapter, "Am I Normal?" refers to your taste in homes and colors. During the course of building a home, there are thousands of decisions to be made. If you plan to have your home appeal to the majority of the home buying public, you need to preface every decision with the question: "Am I normal?" Do most people like this style house? Do most people like this color siding? Do most people like this color brick? Do most people like this type of shingle? Do most people like this color and style cabinet? Do most people like this color countertop? Do most people like this type of lot in this location?

Are my tastes in location, lot, style, size, and layout the same as most people? If the answer is no, consider your choices carefully. The choices you make that step outside the mainstream could be very costly. For this reason, you may want to wait until later in life to build that house. That is, if you're adamant about doing something unusual in your home, incorporate those unusual choices in the home you intend to spend the rest of your life in. For the house you are building now for resale, make a sacrifice and use your second or third choice, which most people agree with.

In the decision-making process of building a home, there will be many times when you ask yourself: "Do I choose the one I want or the one I think will be more profitable?" This is always a tough choice. Consider your objectives. Do you invest money in things you like or things you believe to be profitable? I'm not suggesting that you build a house you are not happy with. You have to be happy with your house. However, I do think that there are levels of satisfaction you can work within. You can still be very happy with your home when the siding or brick color is your second choice. It can still be beautiful to you and the buying public at the same time. You can achieve all of your goals if you weigh the risks and make intelligent, informed decisions.

11

Go Shopping

In order to understand the new home market, one of the most valuable things you can do is to "shop" it. Shopping the market means visiting the builders and communities in your area to see what is out there. I use the term "see" loosely. What I really mean is to understand what types of homes are selling and to analyze the trends.

This task is nowhere near as complex as it may sound. Get in your car with a camera, a pad of paper, a pen, the Sunday "Home Section" from your local newspaper, a map, and a bag lunch. Plan a route that makes sense and visit as many new home communities as you can. Choose the communities that are advertised by the big builders in town, then focus on those in your price range. Check the Web sites of those builders. There are probably other communities that are not advertised. Be flexible and include all communities that are close to your price range.

During your shopping trip, accomplish the following:

1. Visit model homes (on site sales offices) and tell them that you're planning to build a home and are investigating the market. If they're

good sales people, they will be asking you more questions than you care to answer. Be honest about what you're doing (if asked). If they're busy, they will appreciate not wasting time on you. You're looking for:

a.   Floor plan brochures.

b.   A price list.

c.   A list of options (not always available). If they do not have a published list, write down the most popular options and prices. If a list is available, ask what the most popular options are. This tells you what the public is willing to pay for. Take clear notes. After the day is over, you will not remember the details.

d.   Standard features list: This tells you what is included in the base price (i.e., hardwood foyer, raised panel cabinets).

e.   The most popular plan. What is it? Look at the model home and find out what people like about it. What size is it? How many bedrooms? How many baths?

f.   What the sales pace is. Some sales agents paint you a picture of a booming community that is selling quickly. "Quickly" is a relative word. Ask how many homes are sold to date and how long the community has been open for sale. This is simple math and not subject to "spin." The next thing is to determine if that pace is fast or slow. As you visit other communities, you will see what sales pace seems to be the norm. There are a lot of variables that affect sales pace, so do not get too scientific about it. You're just looking for obvious trends.

g.   If the community has hundreds of houses in it already, it's likely to have been there awhile. Make sure your information is limited to the last year of building. The recent option trends, sizes, and sales paces are what you want. Last year's trends do not necessarily apply.

h.   Does the community have amenities (i.e., pool, clubhouse, playground, jogging trail)?

i.   Find out about school systems, shopping, traffic, and quality of life.

j.   What is the average lot size?

k.   Can you buy a lot and build your own house?

l.   Walk through the model home(s) and take note of design elements, room configurations, specification levels, popular colors and styles. Often, model homes are decorated and furnished by professional decorators and reflect the latest styles and colors. Builders often choose popular floor plans for their model homes, so take note of the layout.

2. If there is no model home, there may be a trailer or merely a phone number. You can still get the information you need for **a – k** in the above list.

3. I told you to visit the big builders in town for three reasons. First, they usually have a great feel for the market and you can learn a lot from one visit. Second, the big builders in town are usually in the hot selling parts of town. And third, they can afford to advertise in the paper on a regular basis. This is important so you don't have to drive for three weeks looking. On your way from one community to the next, you will see others that may not have advertised that week (or not at all). Look at those as well. Some communities are developed by developers, and a number of builders build in them. This type of community is often marketed by the individual builders instead of the developer. Sometimes the marketing will be limited to signs in the general area of the site. This is how you will find them. It's important, however, that you find these in your travels, because these developers will sell you a lot directly.

4. Based on what you have seen and the information you've gathered, and ignoring what you LIKE, form an opinion about what side of town is growing the fastest. Form an opinion about what type of house is typical for your price range (size, style, number of rooms, one- or two-story, specification levels, lot size, etc.). Form an opinion about what buyers are looking for (curb appeal, square foot for the money, privacy, convenience, etc.). Form an opinion about what colors are popular these days (ruling out the supertrendy—remember harvest gold?). Make a list of the conclusions you reached.

Take Good Notes

Take good notes before the day is over. Organize them. The form below will help. (You can also download this form at http://books.mcgraw-hill.com/business/download/condon.) Now, clear your head and relax. If you have not already done so, make a wish list of what you want in your new home. Compare it to the list of conclusions that you made from your shopping trip. Are they similar? Identify the differences and work on reviewing and reconciling them. Remember what we talked about in the last chapter, "Am I Normal?"

Shopping List				
Date:				
Questions				
Ask yourself:	Builder Name			
What style of architecture is prominent?				
What is selling more, one-story or two-story?				
Walk through the model home:				
How many bedrooms and bathrooms?				
Is there bonus/flex space?				
Is there any special feature?				
Guess how big it is.				
What colors did the designer use?				
Did I take any pictures?				
Were there any designer features that I can borrow?				
Note the model's layout and room configuration.				
Note the model's specification level if no standard feature is available.				
Ask the agent:				
Is this a growing area?				
Schools, shopping, entertainment, etc.?				

Go Shopping

Shopping List				
Date:				
	Builder Name			
What type of foundation is standard?				
What are the community amenities (pool, tennis, trails, etc.)?				
What is sales pace?				
Most popular plan?				
What about it is nice?				
How many bedrooms/baths?				
Get copies of:				
Plans available.				
Price list for each, including square footage.				
Standard feature list.				
Option list with option pricing.				
Can I buy a lot?				

12

A Borrowed Idea Is a Good Idea

There have only been a few major innovations in architecture in recorded time. The ones that come to mind are the beam, the column, the arch, and the vault. The last innovation was the cantilever. Frank Lloyd Wright pioneered its use. You may have heard of him. Except for the handful of people in history who innovated new architectural elements, every other architect and builder in the world has just been using someone else's idea! They may modify it. They may combine it with other elements, but fundamentally they are employing the same ideas. I'm not saying that designing homes is simple. I'm saying that an "original idea" happens far less frequently than you think. Distinctive design ideas and decorating ideas are usually only new to you. If you're like the rest of us in the world— those of us not on the short list of innovative designers—you need to adapt good ideas that already exist and make them your own.

I keep a file of great houses, designs, and pictures. As I mentioned in a previous chapter, I cut pictures out of trade magazines, other magazines, and the newspaper. I just throw them into my file. Occasionally I will find one idea that works well with another that I found months or years earlier. Combining other parts of a house together with the original idea that inspired me is what I most enjoy about design. Finding a great kitchen or a great master bedroom/bathroom layout is a good starting point for designing your home. They can be combined together with another plan that has a bad kitchen or bedroom. You can cut and paste ideas until you get something that's your own. Getting it to work EXACTLY is quite difficult. This is when an architect or designer is useful. Let them work out the details and you can tell your friends that it was your idea.

When I say borrow an idea, I'm referring to a single design feature in a home, such as a great kitchen layout. If you take a great idea and combine it with others, you create your own work of art. There are copyright laws that protect an entire design. It's important that I clarify the difference between stealing an idea and copyright infringement. You cannot build a plan that you like if it's copyrighted—unless you purchase the plans from the copyright holder. For instance, you may like a plan that one of the builders in town builds. He may have a copyright on it. He has to sell you the plan in order for you to build it. This is not likely to happen. If you modify the print so it is not recognizable as his copyrighted plan, you can build it. There is a fine line here.

If you think about it, how many ways are there to fit three bedrooms, a kitchen, dining room, etc., together? The differences are in the subtleties. Picture a home in your mind that has a foyer with a dining room on one side and a living room on the other. The kitchen and family room are in the rear. Upstairs there is the master bedroom and two other bedrooms. Have I just described a copyrighted plan, or have I just described every two-story Colonial in America? Like I said, there's a fine line. The laws are vague at best. After a law was passed in 1993, the American Institute of Architects stated that "each individual element of a building (doorways, windows, finishes) is *not* protected under the new law. Rather, the design as a complete work is protected. Even though designs are now protected in addition to drawings and models, borrowing of architectural ideas from existing and new buildings is still permitted, as long as the ideas are expressed in the new design in an original manner." They go on to acknowledge that "borrowing and transformation are long-established traditions in architecture." So go borrow some ideas. But to be safe, find a plan you like and buy it, or make substantive changes to an existing plan that alter its character.

I like being inspired by decorator ideas I've seen in other houses. Arches in the walls, niches, and trim features are my favorites. The following are some of the features I put in a few of my houses (you can take a look at them at http://books.mcgraw-hill.com/business/download/condon):

Recessed picture arch. This feature cost me nothing to build. I framed it myself. The trim material was leftover scrap. The drywall contractor was paid by the square foot of drywall, and the arch was included. Framing it requires some skill and an hour or two. If you paid someone for framing and drywall, it might run $100.

Bedroom arch. This feature also cost me nothing to build, and again, I framed it myself. The trim material was leftover scrap. The drywall contractor was paid by the square foot of drywall, and the arch was included. Framing it requires some skill and two or three hours. If you paid someone for framing, drywall, and trim, it might run $200.

Bookshelves. You can build in bookshelves with as little as $53 worth of material and a saw. You can nail the shelves to the wall and paint them in place with the rest of the house. These kinds of bookshelves are nothing fancy, but they will give any house a custom feel.

Foyer square detail. These squares are built with 70 feet of "base cap" trim that cost me 20 cents per foot. The trim man spent a while putting it up because it's ladder work. The material was $24, with probably another $200 in trim and paint labor.

Sculpture/vase niche. Like the bedroom and recessed picture arches, this feature cost me nothing to build. I framed it myself. The trim material was leftover scrap. The extra drywall was negligible. Framing it requires some skill and an hour or two. If you paid someone for framing, drywall, and trim, it might run $200.

Planter boxes. I built these boxes with $127 worth of material and a borrowed saw. Caulk hides a multitude of sins. By the time you caulk them, paint them, and hang them 12 feet off the ground, you can't see any mistakes. We hung ours in a two-story room. I have attached plans for you to borrow.

TV box. Although this project is a colossal pain in the neck, it only cost me $100 for the doors, door slide tracks, and trim material. A trim carpenter and framer might charge several hundred each for the sheer hassle factor, but it's worth it. With a direct vent fireplace below, there is no chimney. This design is very nice for a large TV and VCR, especially if there's a shortage of floor space, as there was in this room.

I saw every one of these ideas in a model home and made them my own. Together with my labor, they cost me $304 in material, my own time and labor, and a small indeterminate cost from my trim and paint subcontractors, who quoted me the whole set of plans and didn't break out the costs. The value that these features add to the house in wow appeal is much more than that. It gives it an expensive custom-built flavor without the expense. I cannot tell you how many compliments I got on those features, and none of them are original ideas. I borrowed them all.

More complicated details can be adapted into more expensive homes. The finishes may be more expensive, but the actual cost of these features is much less than the impact they give.

Here are some other attention-getting design features:

- A tray ceiling with crown molding
- Wainscot made with inexpensive "base cap" trim and chair railing
- Dining room ceiling trim – inexpensive "base cap" trim creates an expensive look
- An ornately trimmed pass through opening in the kitchen
- Built-in bookshelves
- Interior columns to create drama
- A photo gallery – a neat little area upstairs to display the family photos
- Butler's pantry between kitchen and dining room
- Decorative painted wooden headboards and coordinating window valances (great for kids' rooms)
- Cartoon wall murals, great for playrooms or bonus rooms
- Ceiling medallions, great for added interest over light fixtures

A Borrowed Idea Is a Good Idea

You can see these details and more at http://books.mcgraw-hill.com/business/download/condon.

The little details get attention, and people like the details. Incorporate high impact details that look more expensive than they really are. Buyers love to be captivated by neat little features in a home. They remember them, and it helps you sell the home quickly.

13

Pump Up the Volume

The long-standing trend has been toward open, airy designs with fewer walls and more vaulted ceilings. This trend continues to grow. In the not too distant past, eight-foot ceilings in the foyer and throughout the house were typical. Rooms had four walls, one of which had a door or cased opening leading into another similar room. Popular floor plans today have wide-open views of other rooms. Two-story foyers are very popular. Vaulted ceilings, cathedral ceilings, tray ceilings, and even two-story ceilings are popular as well. It is not uncommon for homes to have a two-story foyer that affords a view of most of the rooms on the first floor and out the back of the house. Many bedrooms and bathrooms have vaulted ceilings. This also presents the opportunity for plant shelves at the eight-foot level. Plant shelves are popular in bathrooms, bedrooms, and public rooms. The high ceilings are sometimes referred to as "volume ceilings."

The open floor plans are nice for modern families. From the kitchen sink, you can see the dinette, the family room, and other key rooms where the kids might be playing while dinner is being prepared. The TV in the family room can be seen while cooking or doing the ironing. With the typical family today having two working parents and kids in day care, the precious little time modern families spend together is maximized.

There are several things that can be incorporated into plans that contribute to openness. Using pickets and railings in lieu of half walls opens up the stairway visually. A "half wall" is a 42-inch drywall wall going up the stairs. It's less expensive, but it closes up the room visually. Using several columns in lieu of a wall is also popular. In addition to opening up the plan, columns add elegance. The use of mirrors is a great way of adding depth to a room. Say you have a small living room with a windowless wall that is the primary focus as you enter. You can put ceiling-to-floor mirrors trimmed nicely in painted wood. This doubles the apparent size of the room. Decorators use this frequently with small rooms.

Another growing trend is the use of much more glass. In the past, windows lost a great deal of heat, and too much glass made rooms very uncomfortable in the winter. Now, insulated glass makes windows much more energy efficient, and as a result, homes can use large amounts of glass without excessive heat loss. Innovations in window manufacturing have fueled a window explosion. There are lots more windows, and bigger windows, than ever before. Bringing the outdoors in through the use of windows and glass doors has contributed to the open feeling of today's plans.

Using volume in your plan is highly recommended. Most buyers want it, and most are willing to pay for it. The closed-in plans of yesterday do not sell nearly as quickly as open plans. Volume will help you in several ways:

- It makes your house feel bigger than it really is.
- It impresses potential buyers.
- Since many contractors get paid by the heated square foot, it is a good value. Often, most of the building cost is material only. For example, a painter gets paid $1.40 per heated square foot of house. A 2000 square foot house will cost $2800. If you add a vaulted ceiling in

the family room, the square footage does not change. He still gets $2800. Free WOW factor.

- It will help you sell your house faster and at a better price.

If you're concerned about heating and cooling bills with a high ceiling, it is not a problem. In a very large room, a ceiling fan helps circulate the air. There is some effect on heating and cooling, but it is negligible.

14

Where Do You Live?

What part of the house do you spend most of your time? Think about your daily routine. I generally stay in four rooms: master bathroom, master bedroom, kitchen, and family room. In fact, the other rooms in the house rarely see much action from anyone in the family. My children (both very young) only sleep in their rooms. They spend most of their waking hours with us in our favorite four rooms. Would it surprise you to find out that those four rooms are the nicest four rooms in the house? I chose my house plan for that reason. Most buyers do the same thing. I heard on TV the other day that the average man will spend six years of his life in the bathroom. If that is even close to correct, you can see why it's an important room.

Master Bedroom and Bathroom

Obviously, the master bedroom is very important in a design. It provides a retreat for the parents. In fact, many builders now market it as an "owner's retreat" instead of a master bedroom. Good size and good light enhance its appeal. Wall space is critical to allow dressers, bed, and mirrors. A vaulted ceiling is popular, and plant shelves help add color and interest. And no master suite is complete without walk-in closets. Do not overlook the importance of closet space, especially in the master bedroom.

Many of the same features are popular in master baths: size, light, vaults, and plant shelves. A separate tub and shower are very popular. Big mirrors across the wall help make the bathroom appear larger, so they're well worth the money. A good trick is to put the vanity dead ahead as you walk into the bathroom. The mirror reflects the bedroom, which feels even bigger. Light colors make the room feel bigger. White cabinets are popular, and they help the light feeling. Sunlight really makes a difference in a bathroom. Unfortunately, even large windows get covered up with blinds to achieve privacy. A great alternative that is very popular is glass block windows. With no blinds required, the room is flooded with light, yet privacy is maintained. Real masonry block is harder to install and maintain. I much prefer the acrylic version. It's preassembled, lightweight, and maintenance free.

Kitchen and Family Room

The most important room in the house, however, is the kitchen. Not just the kitchen itself, but the proximity of the kitchen to the garage (for groceries), to the outside (a view from the kitchen is critical), the dinette (right in the kitchen is popular), the dining room (must be attached to the kitchen), and finally, its proximity to the family room. The family room should be in plain view and preferably right next to the kitchen.

The layout of the kitchen is important. The look and feel of it is what most people take note of initially. It does not need to be huge. Huge is good, but not necessary. What most people want out of their kitchen is efficiency and beauty. A light, open, airy feeling is required. Lighter colors give the optical illusion of more space and makes the kitchen feel bigger. Add a big window and a French door and you have a happy place to spend your time. People spend a lot of time in the kitchen, so it needs to be a pleasant place. Although dark woods are beautiful, unless the kitchen is very large, they usually feel smaller than they are. If you choose dark cabinets, install great lighting to keep the kitchen from feeling too dark.

Where Do You Live?

Cabinet space is also important to most people. Having enough of it is critical for two reasons. First, the drawers and cabinets cannot be efficient if they're crammed full and you spend your time digging for pots and pans. Second, what is not in a cabinet usually clutters the counter. This reduces work space and does not look good. Placement of the cabinets is important as well. Wall cabinets contain the dishes, spices, glasses, etc. The efficiency of the kitchen depends largely on the proximity of the cabinets to the appliances and work areas. For instance, if the wall cabinets line one wall, and the cooking is done on the other, the cook will be running around.

The most important aspect of kitchen design is called the "work triangle." If you draw lines on the plan between the sink, the refrigerator, and the stove, you'll see the work triangle. The smaller the triangle, the better. A large work triangle represents the greater distance you would need to travel between these three areas. More distance decreases the efficiency of the kitchen. A compact work triangle means fewer steps to the refrigerator from the stove or sink. (You can see a graphic representation of the work triangle at http://books.mcgraw-hill.com/business/download/condon.)

The kitchen should be open enough to allow for entertaining. During holidays or dinner parties, guests will congregate in and around the kitchen if the design permits. This includes the cook in the conversations and makes it enjoyable. A serving bar or peninsula makes a nice design touch to allow guests in the kitchen without interfering with the cooking.

The family room is the room that most represents how you live. Large or small, it needs to be functional and comfortable. Make sure that furniture fits in a way that is accessible and works for your family. For example, you don't want the couch to be in an awkward viewing location for the TV. Make sure traffic patterns do not cause problems.

No matter what plan you end up building, the four rooms that deserve the most scrutiny are the kitchen, family room, master bedroom, and the master bathroom.

15

Value Engineering

If you're like most people, after considering everything you want in a home and pricing it out, you are way over your budget. The next step is to review everything on your wish list and eliminate those things that are less important.

Most people have a firm budget to work within. If you're over budget, the tradeoff is either size or specification level. For example, if you give up your wish for all brick, you can afford all the square footage you need. The obvious target for cost cuts are the value engineering items in the Master List of Cost Savers you'll find below. Other obvious targets are those that cost more than they appraise for. As discussed in Chapter 9, if an option appraises for $1000 and costs $1500, it's not worth building. After eliminating them, eliminate the features that are not chosen frequently in your market. If screen porches are not frequently built, it may not be the best option to spent money on. Next, eliminate those features that are less important to you than others (either specification levels or room size). Room sizes can be reduced, or rooms can be eliminated.

These choices are the tough ones. Remember to think of it as building an investment. Rely on your business sense.

What Is Value Engineering?

There is always a better way to do things. Construction is no exception. "Value engineering" is a term used to describe the process of refining the product and sometimes redesigning aspects of the product to be more cost effective. Many home-building companies use value engineering to squeeze nickels and dimes out of their products. That may not seem worth the effort, but if you consider the volume of homes built by some of the national builders, the numbers are staggering.

Several of the nation's largest builders build 20,000 or more homes a year. If they use value engineering to save $400 per house, it means an extra $8 million profit per year. Does $8 million sound worth the effort? They are constantly looking for $50 here and $200 there, and their efforts save them millions. Knowing these value engineering items may not save you millions, of course, but it could save you thousands.

In the listing below, we will discuss many of the value engineering techniques used to reduce costs and still provide a quality product. You may not be able to use some of the items on the list. You may not want to. They are not all appropriate in every price range. In fact, some of them are totally inappropriate in certain price ranges. Some even go counter to advice that I gave previously. Choose the ones that make sense for your home and your market. (For definitions of some of the language used in this chapter, check the Glossary in the back of the book.)

Master List of Cost Savers

(For photographs of many of the Cost Savers, go to http://books.mcgraw-hill.com/business/download/condon.)

Reduce the number of exterior corners on the house

Corners are expensive. They produce a lot of wasted material. Four corners are ideal but not always practical (the fewer the better). This is referred to as a "box" (one-story) or a "box over box" (two-story). More corners add visual interest, but it adds cost as well. There are other ways to add visual interest that do not add cost.

Value Engineering

Use a shape as close to square as possible

The area of a square is greater than that of any rectangle with an equal perimeter. This means that you get more square footage for your money when your house is square or close to square. To make my point, I will exaggerate. Imagine a house that is 30 by 30 feet (see Figure 15.1). The square footage is 900. Now imagine a house that is 50 by 10 feet (see Figure 15.2). The square footage of this house is only 500. Both homes have a perimeter of 120 feet that have the same amount of siding, lumber, and drywall. With little additional cost, the closer to square you get, the more house you have.

Lower roof pitch

The steeper the pitch (slope) of the roof, the more material and labor are required to build it. Therefore, lowering the roof pitch (even slightly) saves money on shingles, shingle labor, roofing felt, roof sheathing, trusses (or lumber, if stick built). You may also save on framing labor.

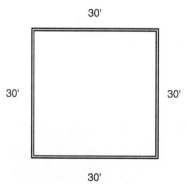

Figure 15.1   Efficiently-shaped home, 900 SF

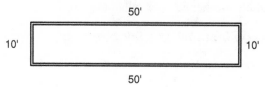

Figure 15.2   Inefficiently-shaped home, 500 SF

Chapter 15

Less expensive window sizes

There are common window sizes that material suppliers stock in their warehouses every day. Uncommon sizes get special ordered. This takes labor, paperwork, and manpower follow-up, which costs money. If you buy the ones that are sitting in his warehouse, they're often cheaper. Be aware of this in the design stage. Architects do not always incorporate standard sizes in their designs.

Fewer windows

Windows cost money. They also involve costs for siding, lumber (i.e., a header), trim, painting, blinds, and final cleaning. Most of these costs are small, but it can add up. Place them well in the room and reduce the quantity. Use a twin window in lieu of a triple. Use a twin in lieu of a bay window.

Less expensive windows

Search construction sites for a window you like. Only look at the large builders in town. They tend to find the good quality, low price windows. Windows vary wildly in cost. You can spend a fortune in fancy little features and special gases in between the glass layers. Do not get sucked in by the hype. Single hung double-pained is typical in most homes these days. Let the house design speak for itself with window SHAPE. Cadillac windows are nice but do not sell the house. Go with the least expensive window you can tolerate. They will not "kill the deal." This opportunity can save you thousands of dollars.

Use home dimensions that minimize waste

This is a tough one, but if you can do it, it saves money. Use floor dimensions that are in four-foot increments so the plywood requires no cuts. Try to keep rooms at 12-foot widths so the carpet will not require a seam. Carpet usually comes in 12-foot-wide rolls. If the room is 13 feet 6 inches, there will be an 18-inch strip cut off another 12-foot roll, and you pay for the whole roll.

Use roof trusses instead of stick building

To "stick build" means to build with individual lumber pieces. Depending on the house you choose and the market you're in, trusses might save you

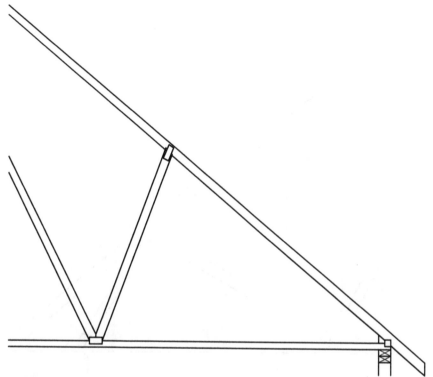

Figure 15.3   Roof truss with tail

money (see Figures 15.3 and 15.4). They are not always cheaper. With a complex roofline, they are expensive. Even with a simple roofline they're often close, but you limit your exposure to theft and misuse on the job site. Framing labor is often less expensive with trusses because they are much faster.

Use eave detail that allows truss tail to hang down

When this happens, the bottom chord of the truss is shorter. This saves money on the trusses (see Figures 15.3 and 15.4). Additionally, you can save between 8 and 10 inches of siding around the entire perimeter of the house. Most houses have this detail now, but a truss plant will design what you send them. Make sure your plans show this (or you knowingly choose something else). Make sure the soffit does not get too close to the tops of the windows.

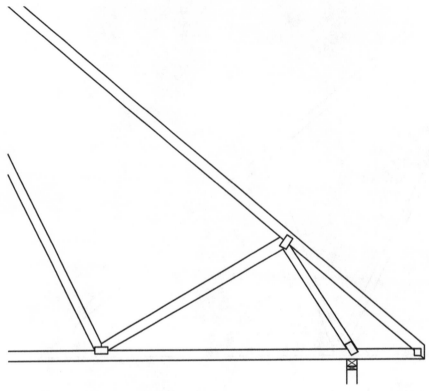

Figure 15.4   Roof truss without tail

Use floor trusses

Like roof trusses, floor truss pricing depends on the plan and the market. It is definitely worth getting a quote. Floor trusses can be open web or wood I-beam. Both are faster than conventional framing (see Figures 15.5 and 15.6).

Simplify rooflines

Many houses have complex rooflines with many gables and changes in direction. Although this is often very attractive, it is also very costly. There is a lot of time involved in framing a complex roof. There is also a considerable amount of wasted lumber and shingles. Simple rooflines are fast and inexpensive.

Simple truss shapes

If using roof trusses, sticking to simple truss shapes will save money. External rooflines affect truss shapes, but so do ceiling heights, vaults, and bearing points inside.

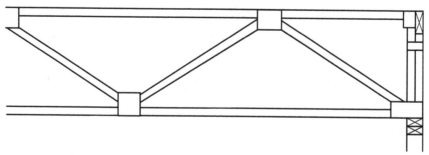

Figure 15.5   Web floor trusses

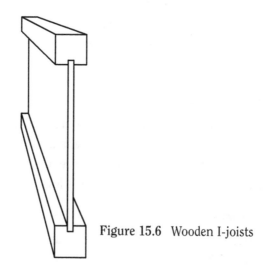

Figure 15.6   Wooden I-joists

Eliminate vaulted ceilings

The cost of vaulted ceilings is low. But when every nickle counts, money can be saved.

Eliminate tray ceilings or box ceilings

Again, the cost of these is low compared to the appeal, but they can save some money.

Eliminate dead spaces in the floor plans

Voids are sometimes created in plans that are less efficient. Each wall of each room should have another room or exterior siding on the other side. If there is dead attic space, or unused space, it costs money.

Chapter 15

Keep walls long and straight

If a framer can stand up a long wall, it saves time and material. Lots of short complicated walls slow everyone down and use more material in framing, drywall, and trim. It can add more money in flooring, shelving, and other trades as well.

Use right angles

Avoid plans with lots of odd angles (45-degree angles are most common). Most plans that use a lot of angled walls are problematic for several reasons:

1. Too much wasted space.
2. Difficult furniture placement.
3. Angled drywall is slow, expensive, and often has finish problems.
4. Lots of wasted material.

Avoid curves

As a general rule, curves of any sort are extremely expensive: curved walls, counters, cabinets, stairs, railings, ceilings, masonry walls, etc. You name it, the costs go up exponentially to curve it. Don't go there. Get your design impact from something else that costs less.

Open floor plans

They sell well and look good. They are easy to build and they cost less. What's not to like? As long as you do not have to use big beams to span large distances, removing walls can save money. For instance, using large cased openings between rooms like the kitchen, dining room, dinette, family room, and living room can open up the feel of the house while saving lumber, drywall, doors, paint, wallpaper, hardware, and door bumps. The rooms can still remain visually separate enough to stop paint colors and/or wallpaper. Eliminating the opening altogether is also an option. You can put the beam or header up in the floor system and run the ceiling straight through the two rooms.

Use shed dormers in lieu of gable dormers

This only applies to the appropriate architectural styles, but many styles accommodate several dormer types. Dormers are always difficult to build, but shed dormers are the easiest to build and use the fewest materials.

Value Engineering

Use dead dormers in lieu of live dormers

Dormers can create a window opportunity in an otherwise useless attic. Although they are expensive to build, adding cheap square footage in an attic is a good idea. "Live" dormers are those you can see from inside the home. "Dead" dormers are strictly for show. You only see them from the outside, and they only add to the exterior appeal of the home. Dead dormers cost less than live ones.

Use attic space for bonus room or recreational room

If possible, utilize attic space. Some plans have complicated rooflines with unknown amounts of attic space available. Others have a simple roofline that begs for a bonus room. If you can afford it AND the house does not get too big for the neighborhood, finish the attic space as a bonus room. Like a basement, it is CHEAP SQUARE FOOTAGE! Think about it. The floor and roof are there already. You're just finishing it off. Some structural changes need to happen, but essentially the structure is there already. Things to consider:

- Stairs to the attic (see next item, "Stack stairs").
- Increase the size of the joists. Ceiling joists are much smaller than if they're floor joists for a bonus room.
- Will you have enough headroom? Many building codes require a certain percentage of the room to be at least a certain height. Appraisers do not count square footage under five feet. Generally speaking, 80 percent of the room needs to have eight-foot ceilings. A collar tie is needed to hold roof rafters together and keep the roof rafters from spreading.
- Allow for enough space between the roof sheathing and the drywall for space for insulation and storage.
- Allow enough space for heating and air-conditioning. Consult an HVAC contractor in the design stage.

Stack stairs

When you put stairs into a house, you lose the space below the staircase. It is a great idea to stack staircases over one another to minimize the lost space. If you don't, two staircases may cost you 140 square feet. Three staircases may cost you 210 square feet of usable space. If you stack them, you have only lost 70 square feet.

Attach the garage

Some plans have detached garages. These cost a lot of money because you have to put siding on four sides of the garage. If attached, the garage has less siding, and it costs less. It also is better for resale. People do not like walking to the garage.

Make the garage integral

There is a difference between an attached garage and an integral garage. An attached garage can be removed. An integral garage tucks under the second floor and cannot be removed without redesigning the house. When this happens, the footprint usually shrinks, which reduces costs. The width of the house usually reduces, which allows you to build on a narrower and cheaper lot. Lastly, two garage walls now abut heated space. That is one less wall that needs siding.

Place bathrooms next to each other

This cuts down on the plumbing material and labor by reducing the length of pipe. If possible, stack bathrooms over other bathrooms or the kitchen. The pipes can run straight up and save time and money.

Two bath vs. 2½ bath

When considering a floor plan, think about using one of the full bathrooms as the public bath in lieu of an additional half bath (commode and sink, no tub). This is easy on a one-story. Three-bedroom, two-bath ranches are common. When the same square footage is considered in a two-story plan, it is highly desirable to have a half bath downstairs. Many one-story plans have 2½ or 3½ baths. Consider eliminating the extra half bath in a one-story.

Eight-foot ceilings in lieu of nine feet or higher

This saves drywall, lumber, insulation, and siding. If you have an open floor plan, the high ceilings are not missed as much.

Make room sizes that will allow optimal use of lumber

Make sure floor joists do not end up being 12 feet 3 inches. If they are, you need to buy 14-foot joists and cut them off. If you make the room 12 feet, you can order 12-foot joists.

Value Engineering

Avoid spanning large open spaces

Bigger spans require larger lumber, which is more expensive. Big beams, structural steel, Lam beams, or large dimensional lumber will dig deep into your budget.

24-inch nonbearing stud spacing

Frame exterior walls and any bearing walls with studs 16 inches center-to-center. Frame interior nonbearing walls with studs 24 inches center-to-center. Any NONBEARING wall can have 24-inch stud spacing. This saves a lot of money without compromising anything. These walls just support the drywall, nothing else. Walls that support loads from above must have 16-inch stud spacing.

Two by fours instead of two by sixes

If your climate will permit, frame exterior walls with two by fours instead of two by sixes. Some climates need two-by-six walls for proper insulation.

Use sliding doors

On doors off the dinette or other secondary exits, the use of a sliding glass door can save money over a regular door with glass. A sliding glass door also provides a lot of sunlight, which can help a floor plan feel open.

Stack bearing

If you think of rooms as building blocks, it's more cost effective to design similar size rooms over one another. For instance, if you put a 10-by-12-foot bedroom over a 10-by-12-foot living room, your lumber costs will typically be less than if the walls do not line up. An ideal design scenario would be for the rooms to all stack on top of rooms of similar size and shape. But don't take this idea too far. It's a goal, not a requirement. If you have it in your head while looking for a plan or while designing one, you can see a plan's potential for savings.

Cut down on beams

When bearing walls do not line up, the solution is often expensive beams. Whether they're made of dimensional lumber or engineered beams, beams can get expensive. Sometimes beams are the only way to make a design work. Other times, you can do something else to change it around. Try to avoid beams if you can. Another problem and potential cost of beams is the difficulty when the plumbers, electricians, and HVAC contractors do their work. They cannot run pipes or wires through beams. This can cause big problems that result in unforeseen expenses.

Eliminate bay windows and small bump outs

Bay windows are attractive, but they are expensive. They can eat up a lot of material and time. They increase material waste and reduce the overall productivity of a subcontractor. When subs see a lot of bays, bump outs, and angles, they often raise the overall price they charge for the house.

Eliminate or reduce porches

Porches are great design features and are nice to have for many marketing reasons, as well as the functional reason of keeping the front door protected from weather. But a large or complicated porch can add a lot of cost. At some point the value of each addition square foot of porch goes way down. Having a nice front porch counts. Having a front porch that is twice as expensive does not count twice as much. Keep front porches to the minimum size required to complete the design intent or to be useful.

Backfill well

Backfill is routinely done incorrectly, and this can cause major structural failure. It may happen right away or it may take a while. Either way, if you're the builder, it will cost you money. Fill dirt in slabs and porches is sometimes dumped into the cavity and pushed down by a bucket on a backhoe or loader. The concrete slab or porch will collapse unless the soil is compacted well. Have a testing agency check it. Fill should be compacted every foot or two during placement using tamping equipment. Masonry or concrete front steps on basements and crawl space houses have a tendency to fall off. They are routinely placed on poorly compacted fill. The weight of heavy steps pulls them away from the house as the soil settles. Backfill and compact correctly.

Minimize header size

Frame all window and door openings with the minimum header size required by code. Code requirements are very conservative. Sometimes, builders or framers will use 2-by-10 headers on every window. This is a waste of lumber. If a two by six does the job, use a two by six. I once had a framer building my house tell me that he would not use anything less than a 2 by 10 in one of his houses. I told him to get out his wallet, drive to the store, and buy some. Do not let contractors steamroll you.

Two-by-four headers

Frame all interior NONBEARING openings with a single two by four turned flat as a header. These nonbearing walls are not carrying weight, so there's no need for a structural header.

Frame stair railings as half walls

Do this in lieu of pickets and a handrail. Half walls are 42 inch drywall walls with a trim cap on top (see Figure 15.7). They are less expensive than wood rails and pickets.

Use prefabricated stair units

The entire stair unit is delivered and set in place fully assembled. This sometimes saves money up front, but its real value is preventing potential

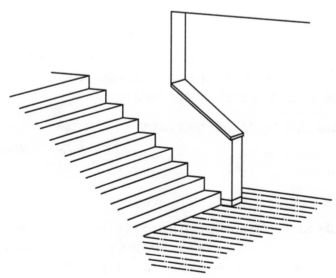

Figure 15.7   Half wall

mistakes and the associated costs. Stair material is a common theft item and the material can be miscut. The biggest problem is getting the riser heights wrong when stairs are job-built. Temporary stair treads are required until the house is trimmed. All of these problems go away with prefab stairs. They are installed at the time the house is framed, and you're done. They are built in a controlled environment and usually squeak less than job-built stairs. They save time as well.

Do not use two stairways

A lot of plans show a secondary set of stairs off the kitchen or in the back of the house. Although this is really neat, I don't ever think it's worth doing. A set of steps takes up about 70 square feet. If you're going to spend the money for 70 extra square feet, spend it on a computer area, a sitting area off the master bedroom, a keeping room off the kitchen, a bigger kitchen, a sunroom, a screen porch, etc. All of these score major points with buyers. The need for a second set of stairs in a big house can be avoided by centrally locating the main stairs.

Panelize

Get a quote to panelize the construction of your home. Instead of the framers building your house on site, a company builds the rough-framed walls in a factory and ships them out to the site. The framers erect the walls in place. Some carpentry work is required to complete the framing, but time and framing costs are reduced. This system also reduces waste a great deal. The potential for job theft and incorrect usage goes down. However, the initial cost is usually higher than stick building.

Eliminate side lights and transoms

They add light to the foyer, but they cost money. Reducing or eliminating them saves money.

One-unit HVAC

Go with the advice of your HVAC contractor on this issue. Ask him if a single unit system will work in your house. Often, a two-story house will get a two-unit system with two thermostats. Depending on MANY factors, this is not always required. A two ZONE single-unit system will sometimes work and save a good chunk of change. You still get two thermostats and separate controls, but you do not have to buy a second unit.

Use a parged block foundation

If you have a brick foundation, you can save a lot of money by using a block foundation (CMU, concrete block). A thin layer of mortar (parging) can fully cover the exposed block surface and create a smooth appearance.

Use a brick front foundation

A twist on the parged block foundation, this method includes a red brick surface on the front of the foundation. The other three sides remain parged block. This saves money over an all brick foundation, yet gives the front of the home a good look. A few well-placed plants on the front corners downplay the material change.

Use one double garage door in lieu of two singles

This saves money on the doors themselves, but also only requires one opener. Two single doors require a wider garage than one double door. You can also save by shrinking the garage.

Keep exterior columns to a minimum

Space columns farther apart on a porch. Put the first column five to six feet from the wall instead of right up against it.

Keep exterior railings to a minimum

If you keep the porch within a certain height off the ground, railings are not required by building code. I have seen builders add $50 worth of dirt around a porch to avoid $400 worth of railings. The extra dirt lowers the height of the porch above the surrounding ground.

Build with local methods

One danger of ordering plans from an architect who lives outside the market is the unusual detail. A plan may have a detail that is typical and inexpensive in another market but unusual and expensive in your market. I was asked to bid a 48-home project with plans from an architect in another market. The foundation details on the plans called for a substantial amount of reinforcing steel and a bond beam. Bond beams are a masonry, rebar, and concrete beam used to strengthen the foundation. They are effective but completely unnecessary in our market. The excessively strong detail raised the cost of the house by thousands of dollars. Make sure that the details in the plans you use are typical in your market.

Use a hip roof on an all brick house

This eliminates the brick veneer up in the high gables. High brickwork is expensive due to the need for scaffolding. Generally speaking, a hip roof is less expensive than a gable roof with brick in the gable. The same generally applies to stucco if it is expensive in a market. This does not apply to a siding house. Siding with a gable roof is generally less expensive than a hip roof.

Use the saltbox shape to save money

This is difficult to explain, but I have found that this shape is VERY cost effective. It markets well too, because the house appears large. A saltbox is a full two stories in front and one story in back (see Figure 15.8). Roof sheathing and shingles are less expensive than vinyl siding, and far less expensive than brick and other more costly exterior finishes. Since the back of a saltbox is mostly roof, the structure is inexpensive to build. It becomes a better value with brick. The downside to this design is a lack of a rear view. However, this is only a downside if you spent money on a lot with a view.

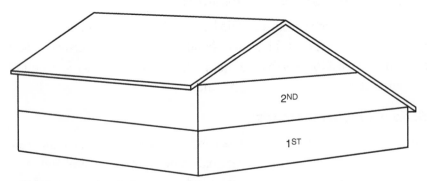

Figure 15.8 Saltbox shape saves money

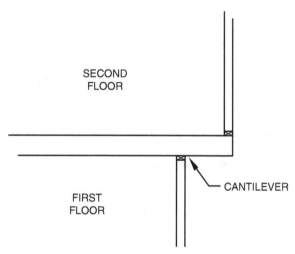

Figure 15.9   Cantilevered second floor

Use cantilevers to optimize your footprint

Foundations are expensive. A cantilever on the second floor will allow you to get more square footage with less foundation expense. In an "all brick" neighborhood, it has another benefit. Since it's impossible to brick the second story of a cantilever (there's nothing to support the weight of the brick), you can use a siding material that is less expensive and still call it an "all brick home." From the front and sides, it is (see Figure 15.9).

Do not drywall the inside of the garage

Sometimes building codes will not allow this, but typically the garage walls that back up to the outside do not require drywall. The ceiling usually needs drywall, and the walls that are insulated (the walls that back up to the house) need drywall. The other walls are often optional. Many markets leave the remaining drywall off.

Do not finish the garage drywall or paint it

Leave the drywall in the garage with only the first "tape coat" of drywall finish. Eliminating the other three finishing steps saves money.

Less brick and stucco

Use limited areas of brick or stucco to provide design interest. Use a less expensive siding material for the rest of the home. A brick area around the front door is nice because guests see it up close when they stand at the door.

Brick veneer first floor only

Use a less expensive siding from the second floor up.

Brick veneer up to the eave line

Brick up to the top of the second floor height and put a roof return (shingle ledge) to cover the top of the brick (see Figure 15.10). Use a less expensive siding material in the gable.

Reduce overhang dimensions on the eaves

This saves on lumber, soffit material (wood or vinyl), and shingles. In some markets, many builders cut the level soffit back to about six to eight inches. Again, this will depend on your architectural style.

Eliminate side overhang on the eaves

Use a two by six nailed tight to the gable ends and wrap it in metal. This saves on lumber, soffit material (wood or vinyl), and shingles (see Figure 15.11).

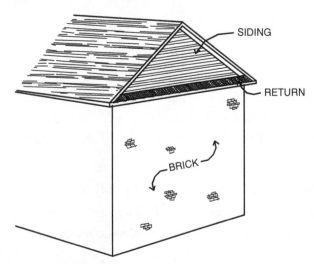

Figure 15.10   Brick veneer up to eave line

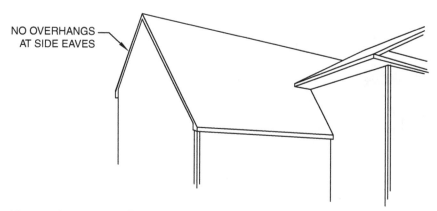

Figure 15.11   No roof overhangs at side eaves

Use four-inch fascia in lieu of six inch

This can save money, depending on the detail. Six inch looks more substantial. If the savings is not worth it, use six inch.

Eliminate as much exterior trim details as possible

Simple saves money. A combination that is very attractive on most plans is to eliminate all trim around windows and use shutters. The trim is hardly missed. Keep the house corners simple, with inexpensive components of whichever siding you choose.

Eliminate pediments over front windows

Some designs can do without the detail, and some cannot. Use your judgment.

Replace pediments over front windows with a less expensive assembly

There are now rot-proof materials that come in standard sizes. Made from cellular PVC, they can be cut like wood into the shape of a pediment and nailed up over a window. They are less expensive than the fabricated pieces. (AZEK is one manufacturer; Website: www.azek.com.)

Eliminate roof returns

Simplify the returns as shown in Figure 15.12 and 15.13 below:

Figure 15.12   Shingled roof return

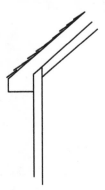

Figure 15.13   Simplified roof return

Use as little wood on the outside as possible

Of course, this will depend on your architectural style. If you can, use vinyl, aluminum, brick, stucco, or any other material that requires little maintenance. This saves on maintenance costs and problems.

Use vinyl siding

Nowadays, vinyl siding is popular in most areas. Some markets still like painted siding, which costs significantly more in initial costs of siding and painting, as well as maintenance costs over the life of the home. If your market accepts vinyl siding, consider it heavily. Six-inch beaded vinyl siding creates a very convincing look of painted siding. For marginally more than regular vinyl siding, it's a nice touch to either set your house above other vinyl-siding homes or to make it look closer to homes with painted sidings.

Value Engineering

Use vinyl soffit

Using vinyl soffit and metal fascia cuts costs up front and down the road as well. There is little maintenance required. Vinyl soffit is appropriate on almost any home. I have it on my all brick home, while many of my neighbors have painted wood soffit/fascia and frieze boards. Theirs cost thousands more than mine, and I never need to paint it or replace rotten wood. Vinyl soffit can be used with painted siding, stucco, shakes, brick, siding, or other exterior coverings. Price all siding options locally to identify values in your market.

Use a concrete patio in lieu of a deck

If your lot will allow a flat area for a patio, this saves money over a deck. Even if you have a small landing and fancy steps down to a patio, you can typically get much more outdoor living space for the money with a patio. A small set of steps right off the door is not very appealing. Consider the transition carefully to avoid it being awkward. Using curved edges is extremely effective. This is easy to form, using strips of quarter-inch luan or other plywood supported by stakes every few feet. As with everything, being different costs money. Don't let subcontractors soak you on this. If the price for curves jumps much, form it yourself. You can always have a carpenter's helper do it for $20 on a Saturday and have the subcontractor pour it at his regular rate. Curves appeal to buyers much more than a rectangle. It's worth the effort.

Use a deck size that maximizes lumber use

If you need a deck, design it to be an effective use of the lumber. A deck that is 12 feet 4 inches will require 14-foot joists and will have joints in the deck boards. Most decking comes in 12-foot lengths. Drawing a deck to fit a 12-foot-4-inch space would cost much more than a 12-foot deck. A 14-foot deck would cost little more than the 12-foot-4 inch deck since you have to buy the longer material anyway.

Place deck stairs carefully

If you can avoid deck steps, that can save money. If the deck is over seven feet in the air, that may be a good idea. If less than seven feet, you probably want steps. Put them on the side of the deck closest to the ground. This reduces the length of the steps and saves money. Stairs can get expensive when long.

Delete gutters

Use a rain diverter over all exterior doors. This keeps water off your head. (If you have expansive soils, follow an engineer's recommendations.)

Only use shutters on the front of the home

In most cases, only windows on the front of the home get shutters. Side and rear windows rarely get them.

Use inexpensive sheathing

No matter what you build or where you build it, there are numerous sheathing materials available for use. Sheathing is the panels of plywood, foam, or other materials that cover the framing on your home. Materials vary in price monthly and quarterly. Many builders use one product all the time and do not take advantage of the price fluctuations. Ask the building supply stores what's available, and use the least expensive material that performs as required by building code AND the roofing or siding materials going over it.

Use OSB in lieu of plywood for roof sheathing

Most of the time, Oriented Stranded Board, or OSB, is much less expensive than plywood. It is also environmentally friendly since it uses small pieces of wood from young trees.

Use OSB on the corners of walls

That is, as structural bracing (required by code), use less expensive non-structural sheathing on the remainder of the wall (if local codes permit). Some areas have extensive stiffening requirements that may prevent this.

Use OSB tongue and groove subfloor in lieu of plywood

Like roof sheathing, subfloor T&G OSB is typically much less expensive and performs quite well structurally. The only performance issue with OSB subfloor is when is gets wet for extended periods of time. If it rains a lot during framing, check to see if the edges have swollen (which sometimes happens with some brands). If so, belt-sand the high edges before flooring goes in. This may seem like a hassle, but the savings for OSB can be WELL worth it. A trick that you can use with OSB and plywood is to drill quarter-inch holes in the middle of puddles after a rain. This gets water off the subfloor before damage can be done.

Use finger-joint studs

That is, of course, if they're cost effective in your area. These studs are made of small pieces of wood, and their cost effectiveness varies. If local availability is there, the price is usually good. They are always straight.

Use small footprints on sloping lots

If you have a lot that slopes, stick with a house that has a small footprint. This keeps the foundation low to the ground. If you use a ranch house on a sloping lot, it can stick out of the ground quite a bit on the low side of the lot. Big foundations kill your profits. A two-story plan limits your exposure.

Use the minimum front setback

Keep the house as close to the street as the building restriction lines (setbacks) will allow. This reduces the length of your driveway and the amount of sod in the front yard. Typically, the sewer and water lines would be shorter as well.

Use one-piece fiberglass tubs/surrounds

"Tile-look" is popular. It looks like ceramic tile on the side walls. Smooth-surfaced tubs are also attractive.

Use CPVC water supply lines in lieu of copper

Copper keeps getting more expensive and other materials keep getting better. CPVC and other materials can be used for the water supply piping. See what is available in your area.

Use single lever production grade faucets

Upgrade to special finishes if you like. Faucets are another area where people sink a lot of money (no pun intended). Well-known manufacturers have excellent faucets in the lower price range. People go to plumbing supply stores and fall in love with faucets that are very expensive. Spend some money on the kitchen sink faucet and the master tub faucet. Save money on the rest. It will not "kill the deal."

Use double lever production grade faucets

Even more of a value, base model faucets with two levers save even more money. Well-known manufacturers have excellent faucets in the lower price range.

Buy appliances yourself

There are great deals out there on appliances. Have the appliances that require connections delivered when the plumber and electrician are there. Make sure they get installed ASAP. They love to walk away. If you're buying a washer/dryer or refrigerator, have them delivered right before you move in.

Reduce cabinet quantity

Reducing the number of cabinets in the kitchen will cut costs. A large pantry closet will offset the lost storage space, and the construction is less expensive. If the kitchen has an open, airy feel with good floor space, the reduced cabinetry will not hurt the kitchen's appeal. (Be careful with this; kitchens are important.)

Less expensive cabinets

An obvious cost savings target is the grade of cabinet. A less expensive cabinet selection will reduce costs as well. It is not always easy to find the cabinets with good pricing. Look at what big local builders are using. Get the name of their supplier. If you go to a retail cabinet outlet, you get pricing that is incredibly high. Never use retail if there are builder sources available. Consumer product surveys say that light color wood cabinets are the most popular. Builders use the following types of cabinets, and they are defined by door style:

Flat panel. Lower price-range cabinet with a flat area in the center of the door. The perimeter of the door has thicker material, while the center panel is recessed in slightly.

Raised panel. The perimeter of the door has thicker material and the center panel has a thick area as well. Typically, the edge of the panel is beveled with detailing and may take many shapes, including square, arched, cathedral, and others.

There are many other door styles, but these two are by far the most popular. Unless MOST houses in your community are different, I would stick with these. The doors and face frames are typically made of oak. Other woods like maple, cherry, and hickory are popular as well. White factory cabinets are typically coated with a covering material and are not solid wood. Most of the frames of factory cabinets are not solid wood. They perform very well and this is not a concern.

Use stock cabinet sizes

Cabinets that have a special size or shape can be quite expensive. There are common cabinet sizes that material suppliers stock in their warehouses every day. Even if they order all of their cabinets for each delivery, the common sizes tend to be the most cost effective. They need to be competitively priced on typical sizes to get business. Uncommon sizes and special shapes are their cash cows. Be aware of this in the design stage, and stick to the basic sizes.

Use a few shorter wall cabinets for variety

This creates drama in a kitchen and can be a positive design feature. Vary the wall cabinet heights to create little pockets for plants or knickknacks.

Use "ventilated shelving" or wire shelving

Wood shelving usually costs more, is not as strong, and requires painting periodically. For a few dollars more than standard wire shelving, a slide bar attachment is available that lets you slide hangers. One exception is the pantry. I like wood shelves in the pantry so small items don't fall through.

Use common marble top sizes

If your home has cultured marble vanity tops, keep the sizes rectangular and not much longer than six feet. Angles and special shapes cost more money because they require more work to prepare the molds. Standard sizes help in several ways:

- The vanity cabinets are standard size and therefore less expensive.
- You may find a bargain at a local home center. Many carry marble tops.
- Many local manufacturers have extras lying around because of mistakes made in the order process. They can be bought at very low prices. Ask the cabinet company as well. They often handle tops in addition to cabinets.

Use standard size vanity cabinets

Much the same as marble tops, choosing a standard vanity cabinet size will keep costs down.

Use a knee space in the vanity

In lieu of two sinks in a vanity, put one sink with a standard size vanity cabinet and a knee space beside it. The knee space is merely a counter that bridges from the vanity cabinet to a wall (or an end panel support made by the cabinet manufacturer; a wall support is less expensive). The whole assembly is typically five or six feet long. The knee space is a makeup counter that a chair can slide under. While saving money, this design is becoming very popular with buyers.

Use laminate countertops in vanities in lieu of cultured marble

Cultured marble tops have integral sinks. When a laminate top is used, a drop-in sink is placed in an opening in the countertop. The use of laminate tops and drop-in sinks typically saves money.

Wrap window openings

With nonwood windows, some material is needed to extend the window jamb from the window to the trim on the inside of the wall. Wood extension jambs are common, and also fairly costly. A less expensive alternative is to wrap the drywall around the corner and back to the surface of the window. Wood stool and apron are nailed at the sill. If a dressier look is preferred, wood casing can be nailed around the window in typical fashion. When the whole assembly is painted with semigloss trim paint, you can't tell the difference between drywall and wood.

Use drywall wrapped openings

A "cased" opening has trim around it. A "wrapped" opening has drywall that wraps around it, eliminating the need for trim. In some markets wrapping saves money. In others the drywall subcontractor charges extra. Compare the two options.

Reduce base size

Using a smaller profile base does save money. Although this is done all the time, I do not think the savings are worth it, because it's highly visible.

Reduce casing size

Using a smaller profile casing does save money. Although this is done all the time, again, I do not think the savings are worth it, because it's highly visible.

Use prefab fireplace inserts instead of masonry fireplaces.

Prefabricated fireplace inserts have been greatly improved in recent years. They're convenient and efficient. Best of all, they're less expensive. You can get an attractive fireplace with any surface, including marble, for thousands less than a masonry fireplace. Of course, the local cost of masonry may make the cost savings vary, but it is usually substantial. Gas logs can be ignited with a flick of a wall switch. Nothing beats the drama of a two-sided (pass-through) fireplace between the master bath and the master bedroom. This is money well spent in a high-end house. Fireplace inserts allow the chimney to be framed and sided since the flue is a self-contained metal pipe. This saves big bucks in most markets.

Shed the fireplace roof

When using a direct vent or ventless gas fireplace unit, a traditional chimney is not needed. A ventless unit has no flue at all because it burns so purely, and a direct vent unit can vent straight out the back of the wall without going up much higher than the mantel. Therefore, when using this type of unit, the roofline can continue down over the fireplace, completely avoiding the expense of the chimney (see Figure 15.14). Note, however, that wood-burning units must have a chimney.

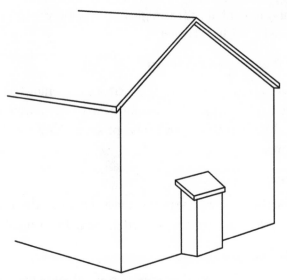

Figure 15.14   Gas fireplace without chimney

Use a modest fireplace profile and mantel

This can save hundreds of dollars and still make a statement in a room. Instead of masonry, marble, or stone on the fireplace surround, use 12-by-12-inch ceramic tiles. I stayed in an apartment during the construction of my last home. It had a direct vent fireplace with tan tiles on the wall, no hearth at all, and no mantel. It still looked great. With limited floor space, the hearth did not cramp the room. It would be equally effective in a smaller home or a small room. An endless variety of colors and styles create personality in a room while saving money. A simple painted wood mantel, or no mantel at all, is acceptable if it fits the feel of the room.

Use Ultralight instead of finger joint base and casing

Ultralight is a relatively new, very inexpensive, and good-quality product. Unlike older, similar products, it nails very well without puckering.

Use hollow core masonite doors

You may have grown up in a house with solid doors, but hollow is the wave of the future. Most homes today are hollow core masonite.

Value Engineering

Use smaller mirror sizes

Wide mirrors in bathrooms are a good investment. It makes the rooms feel bigger. However, you can save a buck by reducing the height. Raise the mirror a few inches above the back splash, while keeping the top at normal height. Since mirrors are priced by the square foot, it's cheaper.

Use steel six-panel exterior doors

Most exterior doors are steel today. They are a good bargain. You can dress up the entry door with side lights. Paintable frames on side lights (glass windows on the side of the door) are an inexpensive way to add interest to your entry. Hardwood doors and side lights are significantly more expensive.

No exterior door glass

Adding glass to any exterior door increases the cost.

Purchase your own lights

Like plumbing fixtures and windows, lights are a great opportunity to make money, and lighting suppliers and electricians have a staggering markup on them. Lights are relatively inexpensive if you shop around at home improvement centers and pick out the bargains. You may buy from four places, but the savings are terrific. There are plenty of very nice fixtures on the low end of the pricing. Take advantage of them. DO NOT spend a fortune on lights. People just do not notice them as much as other things. Get a nice foyer light and a nice dining room chandelier. All other lights should be on par with other houses, or just below. The pricing spread in lighting is huge. A really attractive light might be five times as expensive as a decent light. The decent light will not "kill the deal." Go with that one. Make sure you buy all the bulbs and accessories to go with the lights and ceiling fans. The electricians will not be happy if you forget the down rods on the ceiling fans. Don't forget that a sloped ceiling needs an angle adapter kit when a fan is installed.

Avoid recessed lights

They look good, but they're pricey. Using fewer recessed lights will save money. Surface-mounted lights often light a room better anyway.

Chapter 15

Simplify the lighting plan

Some plans have complex wiring for switches and outlets. Reducing the number of three-way switches and half-hots will save in labor. This translates to money saved.

Size the electrical panel appropriately

Do not specify a panel size. Discuss it with the electrician. Leave a few spare circuits for future expansion. If you randomly pick a panel size, you could pay more than you need to.

Minimize outside decorative lighting

If you put up a ceiling light instead of two coach lights, it saves hundreds of dollars. Ceiling light fixtures are VERY cheap. Coach lights, or other decorative wall-mounted lights, are VERY expensive. Use soffit-mounted flood lights on the sides and rear of the house as needed to provide activity lighting. They are more effective light sources and much less expensive.

If sod is used, limit it to the front yard

This provides instant curb appeal in the front, but the sides and the back get seed and straw. With a few seasons of TLC, you can grow your own and save a good amount. If you're prone to killing anything that is green, like me, install sod. I could not grow a yard if my life depended on it. I sodded my last yard and never looked back.

Use two-thirds sod one-third planting area

This trick saves money on sod. One-third of the sodded areas is mulched with plants or small trees. This ratio works well.

Buy plants in bulk

Landscapers get a substantial professional discount on plants. If you plan to do your own landscaping, go through a wholesale distributor or have a landscaper buy your plants (for a small fee).

Use a mailbox kit

There are kits available in home centers that have everything you need. They're less expensive than buying individual parts, and can be very attractive.

Value Engineering

Use inexpensive hardware with a lifetime finish warranty

There's nothing more irritating than replacing cheap hardware that is tarnished and damaged within the first year. There are plenty of them out there. You can spend a lot of money on high-end hardware. There is a compromise. Kwikset is a manufacturer of high quality interior and exterior hardware with a great finish that lasts. The Valient Series is cost effective and very reasonably priced. Lever handles are also available for a more elegant look.

Avoid unusual fixtures, finishes, or specifications

Unusual almost always costs money. Showrooms have stock on the floor that involves little effort to sell. If you want something out of a catalog, it involves time, follow-up, and hassle. This translates to money. Order what is readily available OR ask the right questions to ensure that it's not costing money.

Ask others to value engineer

Every contractor who bids on your house can tell you valuable ways of saving money. Every supplier who quotes material prices can tell you about less expensive materials, or better ways of using material. Ask questions of everyone involved and then listen carefully for savings opportunities.

Shop for clearance items

Almost everyone makes mistakes when they order material for a customer. Those mistakes often sit in their facility gathering dust and taking up space. They usually welcome the chance to dump the spare material at a hefty discount. Do not redesign your house around a remnant, but they may have something that will work. Cabinets, counters, doors, trim, windows, shingles, siding, plants, bricks, retaining wall blocks, plumbing fixtures, lights, appliances, ceramic tile, and flooring are all prime suspects.

No glass in garage doors

This saves some money, and a lot of people like the security and privacy.

Fewer garage bays

Eliminating the garage or reducing a double garage to a single garage will save a lot of money. In some markets garages are optional.

Use an uninsulated garage door

Depending on your climate, you may be able to use the less expensive uninsulated garage doors.

Eliminate medicine cabinets in bathrooms

Depending on the style, eliminating these can save a lot.

Use aluminum columns on porches

Save some money now and a lot of money later. Maintenance on wood columns is expensive. Aluminum is maintenance free.

Frame 24 inches on center

A fairly complicated method of saving money, this method spaces ALL roof, wall, and floor framing members on 24-inch spacing. All members are stacked to transfer the loads directly to the foundation. Design work is required to execute this method.

Remember, I do not recommend the use of all of these cost savings ideas in every circumstance. Sometimes it's worth the extra money to produce an attractive and marketable product. You need to select the ones that might save you money without hurting your ability to market the house later.

Another good source of cost-saving ideas and value engineering is the subcontractor force bidding your house. As you solicit quotes from builders, subcontractors, and construction managers, ask them if they have any cost savings ideas. They will help you.

Choose a Cost Effective Style

There are many ways to save money by value engineering, but curb appeal is sometimes compromised. A great way to approach value engineering is to choose a simple and stately architectural style that is cost effective to nail the details. I personally find the simple Colonial homes very attractive. Georgian in particular (see Figure 15.15) is very elegant while also extraordinarily efficient. You can spend money on some fine entrance detailing and still be well below the cost of homes of comparable size.

Figure 15.15   Georgian home

This Georgian home sold for the same price per square foot as adjacent homes, yet it has many cost-saving design traits. Notice the following value engineering:

1. The foundation is close to square, which maximizes square footage per linear foot of exterior wall.
2. The roof is hipped, which eliminates high gable brick.
3. The garage is integral, minimizing brick expense.
4. There is minimal porch expense.
5. The lot is flat, which eliminates any wasted expense on foundation. The lot 100 feet away is a cliff.
6. There is only detail on the front windows.
7. There is a simple roofline.
8. There is a simple yet appropriate front door.
9. There is no masonry chimney.
10. There are no side lights.

11. Unlike most neighboring homes, there is no stucco detailing around the windows.
12. They used a double garage door in lieu of two singles.
13. The rooms stack neatly.
14. There are no bay windows or bump outs.
15. There are only four corners on this house.

16

Do It Yourself

A great way to save money when you build a house is to do some of the
work yourself. There are many things in your average house that anyone can do with a little training. A little guidance and some insight into
tricks of the trade, and you're ready to do it yourself. If you don't believe me,
look at programs like Habitat for Humanity. They have built tens of thousands of houses worldwide using mostly unskilled volunteer labor. All you
need is a little guidance. You can get that from many sources, including reference guides, home improvement TV shows and their Web sites, home
improvement stores, material suppliers, contractors, and subcontractors.

Wherever you buy the material is the most likely place to start. Go to
the place the contractors do, like a tile supplier. Most of the time they'll
talk to you as long as you listen about the right way to install their product. You can learn a great deal from them (sometimes too much). They
will tell you the best tools to use and other time-saving tricks. Home
centers will sometimes do the same, if you can find someone. I find that
the professional suppliers are a much better source.

If you're having a builder build your home, remember one thing: He'll tack on a markup to any work performed under his contract. Builders have real overhead costs, and they are entitled to that markup. However, from your point of view, overhead and profit can add up quickly.

We have already talked about a number of ways to save money in design. Now let's look at how you can do some work yourself, and how this will save you money. You'll not only save the amount of the labor, but you will also save the builder's markup. Some builders are marketing home buyers' work as "Sweat Equity." Buyers can do some of the work themselves to save money.

Sweat Equity Work

Here are some of the things you can do yourself:

- Install insulation
- Paint
- Wallpaper
- Landscaping
- Final cleaning

With very little instruction, anyone can do these phases of work if they're willing to get dirty and get it done. As a builder, I can tell you that Sweat Equity is a pain in the neck! Builders are on a strict timetable; they have interest adding up with every day that passes. When the house is ready for insulation, it needs to happen THEN. If the buyer does not get right on it, the builder is losing time.

If you want to pursue Sweat Equity with your builder, commit to him that you'll get it done within a given time frame. If he still is not comfortable, tell him he can get his own subcontractor to do it after so many days if you fail to get it done. This will allow him a reasonable time frame to work with, and he may be more receptive. (By the way, I use the term "he" for a builder, but of course it could be "she" as well.)

Work You Can Do During Construction

If you're managing the construction of your home, there are many things you can do yourself. I hear people tell me occasionally that they're building their house a little at a time over the years. I guess, in these situations, that money is not borrowed, since the interest would eat them alive.

This section is directed at the working stiffs out there who are building a house during a work week. I have weekends and after-work hours to supervise, schedule, order material, and do whatever work I can get done. These are things that are easy to do and will keep the costs down:

Trash control. Daily trash policing and sweeping is necessary. Put trash in a container and have it removed when space is needed. I like a trash bin made of four sheets of plywood (eight feet square and four feet tall). A typical house will need three to five trash removals during the construction process. The grader can do it.

Selective clearing. Depending on the type of trees in your area, some light tree trimming and thinning out of the woods is often necessary. The undisturbed areas around the house may need to be thinned out. If you do it up front, the grader can remove the debris when he's doing the heavy work. After the surveyor locates the house in the woods, thin out the areas outside the footprint and throw the debris inside the footprint of the house. It saves a bunch of hauling at landscaping time.

Silt fence and erosion control measures.

Material management. Sorting good and bad material nightly will save you a LOT of money. You would not believe what gets thrown out on a job site. If you sort and stack lumber and other material, the cut pieces will get used, and the lumber goes much further. Sometimes the good lumber will lay sideways through a puddle for six days until it warps. This is when the framer tells you the lumber you got him was "bad."

Burn trash, wood, and paper. If burning is permitted in your area, keep a burn pile of the tiny cut pieces to burn. Subcontractors will keep warm one way or another. I find eight-foot studs in fires all the time. It's best to keep some kindling around. If you keep up with it, the trash you remove will only be the toxic items that cannot—and should not—be burned.

DO NOT burn the toxic items. By "toxic" I mean anything other than natural wood and regular paper fumes. Plastics, tar paper, adhesive containers, and other nonwood items are very bad for you. If you think you do not inhale any, smell your clothes the next day. You cannot help but inhale the toxins. It is definitely not kind to the environment, and I think it is also illegal. DO NOT BURN PRESSURE-TREATED WOOD. IT IS POISONOUS! It contains *arsenic*. The smoke is toxic. Concentrated arsenic in ashes can also kill after the fire is out. If a child ingests the ashes while playing in the yard, it can be deadly.

Grade inside the crawl space. This is typically light shovel and rake work.

Custom framing features. If you're considering any of the features I discussed in Chapter 12, "A Borrowed Idea Is a Good Idea," or some other idea that requires detail framing work, I suggest you do it yourself. Most of it is not that difficult; it's just very slow work. Framing crews will charge you more than it is worth to do it. The lead man does the work while four other guys stand around costing him $60 per hour. You pay for all of them. I did all my custom rough framing work with a circular saw and a jigsaw. Everything else is just patience, careful measurement, and geometry.

Fire caulk or air seal. Caulk all penetrations through the floors and top plates with fire caulk and air seal. Air sealing is caulking all sills to the plywood, all studs together, and all windows and doors to the wood.

Speaker wire. While the walls are open, run speaker wire to any room you want. Make sure they are inconspicuous. Also make sure you get the right size wire. I learned the hard way. If the run is too long, you lose power. (By the way: Never drill through a truss member or an engineered beam.)

Attic storage. Before the drywall is up, put some plywood in the attic for attic storage. Remember a few things. Block up the plywood so insulation will fit under it. Some insulation needs 10 or more inches. Also remember not to overload the ceiling joists. If you have trusses, consult the manufacturer. $\frac{7}{16}$" OSB is not thick enough for attic storage. Use $\frac{23}{32}$" OSB.

Insulation. This is very easy to do. It's just unpleasant. I choose to pay someone else to do it. Wear long pants and sleeves. Wear a mask and eye protection. The fiberglass irritates the skin, eyes, and lungs. If you're dressed well for it, there's nothing to it.

Do It Yourself

Drywall is best left to the professionals. I once started to finish my bonus room. I had to pay more for someone to fix my mess than it would have cost to start with. It's harder than it looks to finish big areas.

Special trim. There are some custom trim ideas in Chapter 12. Whether it's those or some other idea, make them ahead of time. Install them when the trim carpenter is trimming the house, and the painter will paint them in place. If you can take a day off, or have the trim subcontractor come on Saturday, you can use his tools to build the shelves or other items. I went to the house my trim man was working on the Saturday before he came to my house. I used his tools. He offered advice, because I looked like I needed help. I built my stuff and put it in the house later that week after work.

Chair rail or crown molding. To keep trim labor costs down, you can do the crown and chair. I said it before: Caulk will hide a multitude of sins.

Deck. If your house needs a deck, pour the footings with the main house. Put the band board and flashing against the house so the siding subcontractor can finish his work around it. This buys you time to put the deck on whenever you have time. I recommend finishing it before landscaping so you don't destroy the grass. You can do both after you move in if you want.

Landscaping. If the yard is graded properly, there is nothing to landscaping. Dig big holes and use planting mix for your plants. Lay the sod yourself. About half the cost of landscaping is the labor. Other than designing, it isn't that hard. It does take some research to put the right plants in the right location. If done incorrectly, it looks terrible and unprofessional. Go to a local nursery and get all the advice they will give you. Follow it. Find out where the landscapers buy their plants and sod. Buy direct from them and save a fortune. I found that nurseries that cater to the general public are marked up three to four times wholesale prices. One word of warning: I installed about 120 Indian hawthorn shrubs around my second house. I soon found out that it is a delicacy among the local deer. I considered taking up hunting.

Ceiling fans.

Wallpaper, boarders, or faux finishes.

Blinds. In most homes, white vinyl miniblind in almost every window is a good idea for privacy. They are available at home centers and the very inexpensive ones work just fine. They look good and do the job. If mounted inside the window opening, they do not interfere with drapes or other window treatments. If more expensive blinds are required in a more expensive home, I find that professionals are needed to custom make them.

Screens.

House numbers.

Mailbox.

Fences.

Garage door opener.

Something I do all the time is borrow a helper from a professional contractor. Most construction people are very open to earning a few extra dollars on the weekend or after work. They have the skill AND THE TOOLS, and you have the cash. There are pros and cons to this. The pros are that you get it done cheap. The con is a lack of responsibility and warranty. If the tiles crack, will the helper come fix it for free and buy the new tiles to do the work? I doubt it. But I think it is usually worth the risk if the person is recommended. You can save a fortune in labor and in tool rentals.

Depending the amount of free time you have and the size of your house, you can do some or all of these things. I must warn you not to overcommit. There's a lot of work needed just to manage the construction. Don't base your budget on HAVING to do all this work. That way, if you run out of time, you won't be over budget when you hire someone. Depending on the type of financing you have, you might be able to do many of these things after you move in. Don't be afraid to jump right in. It's therapeutic to work out your frustration. The more you do, the more you save. Think of it this way: Would you do this stuff if someone paid you? You ARE making money. It is just delayed payment. You get paid for your work when you sell your home.

In addition to saving money, it makes for good conversation at dinner parties. I get comments all the time on things that I did. A comment like "nice patio" turns into a ten minute discussion about the day my three-year-old son "helped me" lay the stone pavers. Its fun to remember all the work in hindsight. It makes you glad you did it.

17

Decorate for Resale

As we discussed earlier, most people sell their house within a few years, even if they plan to stay in it. If you plan to sell it, this chapter is even more important. Decorating your house with the intent to appeal to the majority of the buying public is a great way of making money. Your house will be more appealing to more people when you put it up for sale. More appeal means a higher sales price.

Inside the House

Light colors and earth tones are very popular. Off white or beige is a good color selection for carpeting, paint, and even countertops. White cabinets or medium color wood cabinets are always good sellers. Variations of gray are also popular, but they sometimes feel cold.

When a contract falls through on a home under construction, the first question builders ask is: "What colors did they choose?" The answer that we don't want to hear is: "Pink counters, green floors, and burgundy carpet." That house is sure to sit there for a LONG time waiting for someone to buy it. Builders will often replace the carpet or counter because they know it will sit and cost them money. If they do sell it, they have to discount it heavily. This is what you want to avoid. You may have a knack for decorating. You may be able to make that color scheme look fantastic. You may just want a more conventional combination of some bold yet tasteful colors. Someone in this world has your same taste, but MORE people like subtle earth tone and white. Stick to those.

If you want to add bold color to a room, you can do it with artwork, furniture, plants, throw rugs, wall hangings, sculpture, window treatments or other means. What do all of these items have in common? THEY GO WITH YOU! What stays with the house is ONLY what the buying public wants.

Painting a room deep blue or hunter green is not the end of the world. You can paint it purple with a Barney motif if you want. A coat of paint when you go to sell the house is pretty easy. Most people cannot envision the house after a paint job. They tend to see what's there. Paint before you sell. Let me give you an example.

The first house I bought was previously owned. It had an orange kitchen that opened into a HOT pink dining room. The dining room had pink-tinted mirror squares glued to one whole wall. The dining room was wide open to a purple living room. The carpet was yellow. All of these colors were plainly visible from the foyer. It was crammed chock full of stuff, knickknacks, oversized furniture, and general junk. Needless to say, it sat on the market so long that the buyers slashed the price, and I got a great deal. A week of mirror stripping and painting gave me a bigger house than I could otherwise have afforded. And it was now all white and beige. I saved enough on the purchase to buy new carpet. (I paid a carpet guy on the side to do it one Saturday, and paid him cash.) How much more do you think those sellers would have gotten for the house if they had painted before it went on the market?

If you do a road trip and shop the model homes, ask them what the popular colors are. See for yourself. Do not necessarily go by what's in the model home. They are often fairly bold design statements.

Decorating for resale is not just colors. Clutter is bad. Before you sell, pack some stuff. Simplify. Less is more. This makes rooms feel bigger.

One final point on color: Be wary of trendy colors. I will leave you with these two thoughts: Harvest Gold and Avocado Green.

Outside Decorating

Making the outside of your home appealing is just as important as the inside. Make sure that your exterior color scheme is one that most people like. Driving through new communities can tell you a lot about this.

Builders find that people want the same few colors all the time. The particular colors vary with location and product, but there's usually a fairly small group of VERY popular colors and a larger group of colors chosen fairly frequently. Do not get outside that group. You don't want to have an unusual exterior color. It is expensive if not impossible to change. You turn off buyers before they even see the inside of the home if you have an unpopular color. Remember, appeal to the widest group possible.

Here are some examples:

Vinyl siding. White, tan, dark tan, and cream are winners in most places. Yellow is getting on the fringe. Light blue and pink are way off base in most markets, unless pastels are popular.

Brick. Shades of red and brown typically are popular. Pink tones in the brick can look great, but resist the urge. Some people can't live in a pink house.

Stucco. Colors for stucco tend to vary by region. Stick to the VERY popular colors. The wide variety of possibilities gets some people in trouble. Earth tones and subtle colors are a good choice, unless pastels dominate the market.

Painted siding. Like stucco, follow the market. Stick to earth tones for your best bet.

Remember to coordinate your shingles with your siding. There are shingles that coordinate with brown and tan colors, and there are black shades that go with almost everything. Tile and other special roofing can coordinate as well. Consider this early because you will be installing shingles in the first third of the project.

Coordinate your exterior colors well. If this is not your strength, GET HELP. Ask at least five people with good taste.

Chapter 17

Landscaping is an important decorating consideration because you want it to look GREAT when you sell it. The problem is, you don't know what season you will sell it in. If you sell it in the winter, will the yard look dreary and lifeless? Do you live in a climate that has seasons? Most of us have ugly times of the year.

I like to use evergreen trees in my landscaping. That way, if I sell it in the winter, I have green trees in my yard and not leafless twigs. For those of you who don't have green thumbs, evergreen trees/plants do not drop their leaves in the winter. Not all evergreens look like Christmas trees. On the contrary, there are many varying shapes and sizes with different leaf colors and textures. I like having some holly trees and wax myrtle trees in key locations. Remember, you want to stand out among your competition at resale. What better way than to have green trees when theirs are gray and lifeless? If you live there forever, it's still a good thing to do.

18

Rental Properties

What Makes a Good Rental House?

It varies everywhere. In my town, it's a 1200 square foot house in a good school district with three bedrooms, two baths, a garage, and a decent yard. A fenced backyard is a plus but not required.

There are definite target rental rates you want to hit. Above a certain dollar amount per month, your pool of potential renters drops dramatically. Where did I learn this information? I asked local property managers and other rental investors. (We discuss property managers later in this chapter.) Ask them what the "perfect rental house" is in your market. Ask where that rental should be. Obviously, you need to be where new construction is possible. Once you know what rents and what doesn't, use the strategies in this book to find the perfect house that fits the rental profile AND will sell well when the time comes.

Why worry about selling if you plan to rent it? Sometimes a dynamic in the market will justify the sale of a rental home. Maybe school districts change, or a highway is being built nearby. For many reasons, rental properties also need to have the best possible chance for a quick and profitable sale if needed. The only difference in the process is that not all houses that sell well rent well. Answer the question about what rents and then it is exactly the same process.

In the very first chapter we talked about keeping your emotions out of the decision-making process. If you're building rental properties, there is a different challenge regarding emotions. It is way too easy to focus on rental properties that reflect *your* lifestyle, taste, needs, and economic position. Remembering that you are not the renter is very important. Keeping the ego in check will allow you to build the houses that the renting public wants, and it will allow you to make the most money possible with each opportunity.

At Least Break Even

Many rental investors have told me that their target is to break even on rent and mortgage. They say that taking a loss for the maintenance is acceptable and that building equity is more important than making money each month. When paying retail for houses in some markets, this may be all that's possible.

My strategy allows you to find the houses that cost so little that you can also make money every month. Make sure you look at this closely before you build. In Chapter 1, remember, we also talked about the importance of having enough rent left over after paying the mortgage to provide an income.

Who Rents, and Why?

All kinds of people rent for many reasons. But there are three types that are noteworthy for this discussion:

1. Some renters have terrible credit and cannot buy a house. Late payment and missed payments are obviously not desirable. This is why a credit check is mandatory.
2. Some renters have an old bankruptcy or other credit problem that they're recovering from. If the problem is behind them, they could be good long-term renters for you as they restore their credit.
3. Some people are just not ready to buy a home yet. If they rent yours long enough, they may want to buy it.

Property Management

In the beginning, it is not hard to manage your own rental properties without interfering with your regular full-time job. At some point, however, it may become necessary to have a property manager. For a fee, a property management company will coordinate maintenance and repairs, handle leasing and evictions, collect rent, and pay bills. That fee may be 10 percent of the monthly rent. This can add up quickly, so only do it if you can't manage them on your own. Partial services are also available from property managers. They can find tenants, do credit checks, qualify them, and write a contract for a fixed "finder fee," which might be something like one-half the monthly rental rate.

Placing tenants is 80 percent of the headache in rental property. Depositing rent checks is easy. Repairs are fairly infrequent since the houses are new. Many property managers have a handyman type person they use for maintenance and repairs. If you send them enough finder fees, they may share him. If not, find an apartment maintenance person who wants some side work. They all do. For major work, rely on your subcontractors. They can do work for much less than a property manager.

Cash Flow

Good property managers have little patience with late payments. Evicting a tenant is made easier in many states through good laws and help from law enforcement. Understanding the eviction process and filing for eviction quickly can save you from costly delays. Filing that notice gets a late paying tenant's attention and may resolve the problem without further delay.

Saving money for maintenance and vacancy will prevent cash flow issues. Obviously, the goal is to keep a tenant in the property at all times. In between tenants, you may need to make a payment or two. New carpet every few years, landscaping issues, paint, and caulking will be required. Save enough money from the rent to pay for these repairs.

Set Up an LLC

Ask an attorney how to protect your personal assets from the rental property business in your state. Mine suggested setting up a Limited Liability

Corporation. In an LLC, homes are owned in the name of the LLC and not deeded personally. Taxes are done separately. A separate bank account keeps the money separate.

Ask your attorney about any other laws in your state that may have an effect on how you run your business. Find out if you need to be licensed.

For more information...

There are several books on property management that will give you further insight. Here are a few:

1. *Streetwise Landlording & Property Management: Advice on How to Own Real Estate and Manage It Profitably*, Weiss, Adams, 2003
2. *The New No-Nonsense Landlord*, Jorgensen, McGraw-Hill, 2003
3. *Property Management for Dummies*, Griswald, For Dummies, 2001

19

Who's Doing the Building?

In this chapter we will discuss the nuts and bolts of contracting and building a home. You may be managing the construction and hiring the subcontractors yourself. You may hire a manager. You may choose to hire a builder and let him worry about it. Regardless of the direction you choose, understanding the process is a critical step toward keeping your sanity and running a well-planned and well-executed construction process. Let's discuss each one of the options.

Hiring a Builder

Hiring a builder to build your house is certainly the easiest way of going about it. You can still make a good profit on a home if it is designed well and you follow the strategy, but hiring a builder will eat up some of the profits. The builder assumes the risk and is entitled to some of the rewards. If you hire a builder, choose the right contract to maximize your profit (see Chapter 20, "Contracting").

All builders are not created equally. Do a lot of homework on a builder. Get references and talk to them. Get the names of the last 10 houses they closed, not the list of people they want you to talk to. As a builder, I can assure you that the buyer's opinion of a builder is not always a complete and fair assessment. What is important is that you identify any trends. If many say that the builder is unresponsive and communicates poorly, there is probably truth to it. If one person in 10 has a horror story, weigh the facts, and ask the builder for their side of the story. How they talk about problem customers will give you a good insight into their commitment to customer satisfaction.

Acting as Your Own General Contractor

It is called many things, including acting as your own general contractor, being your own builder/contractor, being the construction manager, etc. Whatever the term, it means that you are the responsible party building the home. You pull the building permit in your name and assume the liability. The subcontractors work for you and you pay them directly. In some states home-owners can build their own home without being a licensed builder. There are often conditions attached to this privilege, limiting the frequency with which you can do this and controlling the plan approval process. Check with your local building inspection department to see what the requirements are.

I've known many people who have done this. All of them were happy with the results. I must caution you, though: There are some serious risks involved building this way:

1. You are liable for the costs of all mistakes made during construction.
2. If you sell the home, you are liable for any latent defects for a period of time (often 10 years) just like a builder would be.
3. Theft, vandalism, material misuse, and other expenses are usually absorbed by the builder. You absorb them doing it this way.
4. What you don't know CAN hurt you. A rookie error can cost unbelievable money if it is a big one. Or worse yet, some mistakes are not reasonably fixed. For example, the first floor is too close to the ground to properly drain the yard. What do you do, raise the house?
5. Subcontractors may leave you after they get their check and never return.

Who's Doing the Building?

These are some of the risks builders assume when they build your house for a fixed contract amount. They offset these potential liabilities with the profit they make. You can reduce the cost of construction substantially if you carry these risks and manage construction yourself. Good drawings, good planning, good subcontractors, and thorough inspections will reduce the possibility of mistakes. Keep in mind, however, that houses rarely get built without mistakes. They are built by human hands in the hot sun, rain, and snow. Even the best builders find and correct mistakes during construction. You first have to find them. If you don't know what you're looking at, you cannot detect the mistakes.

I said earlier that all of the people that I know who built their own homes were successful. I'm quite sure that this is a statistical anomaly. I know there are horror stories out there. I just don't know those people. Many that I have known were in some form of the construction business—not necessarily builders, but suppliers, sales agents, office staff, and others associated with the industry. Others who are not in the business, like my grandfather, have also done well. They tend to be handy people by nature and are not afraid to get dirty or ask a million questions. In fact, if you are not willing to get in the trenches to figure it out and get it done, this is not for you.

For more information…

There are several reference books that will spell out exactly what you need to know about construction materials and methods. They will provide you with the technical background necessary to act as your own general contractor or build your own house. Here are a few:

1. *The Complete Guide to Building Your Own Home*, McGuerty & Lester, Betterway Books, 1997
2. *Housebuilding – A Do It Yourself Guide, Revised and Expanded Edition*, DeCristoforo, Sterling, 1977
3. *Do It Yourself Housebuilding: The Complete Handbook*, Nash, 1994

Check with your local building inspection department to find out about the rules in your area regarding building it yourself. Most of the people who can build it themselves have no doubts that they can handle it. If you still have doubts after reading a reference book, hire a builder. Know your limitations and work within them. You can still apply all of the principles in the book, hire a builder, and make a great investment.

Hiring a Manager

Hiring someone to manage the construction of your home is sometimes a good compromise. A manager can do much of the active management of the project for a set fee. The manager is not responsible and carries no risk. Therefore, a reasonable fee is a good deal for both the manager and you. Since the manager carries no risk, that means you carry it. The responsibility for problems is part of what a general contractor's fee pays for. That responsibility falls on you in this arrangement, so the fee can be reduced. You need to understand the process fully and make sure everything happens as planned, but this arrangement allows someone with limited time or limited construction knowledge the opportunity to build their own home and save money.

The arrangement can be essentially this:

1. The Manager consults on plan and lot selection.
2. The Manager does estimates, bid preparation, bid solicitation, and review.
3. The Owner selects the subcontractors/vendors from the list.
4. The Owner secures financing and handles all payments.
5. The Owner secures insurance for the project.
6. The Manager gets the permit, handles building inspections and code compliance.
7. The Manager schedules the work.
8. The Manager handles quality control and punch lists.
9. The Manager resolves disputes and problems.
10. The Owner feeds the Manager with material/product and color selections.
11. The Manager receives a modest fee or a percent of the cost of construction.

Who's Doing the Building?

If your state requires a builder's license, a licensed manager may be the only way you can build it yourself. Since the permit holder is usually held legally responsible, the manager will need to be held harmless in a legal agreement.

A word of warning: When you relieve them of responsibility, consider the ramifications. You need to be confident in their abilities and stay on top of them. Have an attorney draw up the documents and protect your interests.

Becoming a Builder

If this book's strategy sounds like something you plan to latch onto tightly, you may consider getting your builder's license. It may seem crazy, but ask how difficult it is.

Each state has an agency that licenses builders. They can tell you the licensing requirements. It is often as easy as passing a test and paying a licensing fee. There are prep courses available that tell you how to study for the test. If a few evening classes and some studying does not scare you, your best bet may be to get licensed. Some states require bonds and other stipulations that make it more difficult or costly, but I recommend looking into this option. If you think you may build a few houses for yourself over the next several years, it may make even more sense.

Let Someone Else Build it!

As I said back in Chapter 3, "Cheap Dirt, Dirt Cheap," cash flow is the name of the game in building. No cash, no business. When a builder has a house sit for a long time, it can cause cash flow problems because he has so much money tied up in it. Cash flow is not a problem for some builders, but if you see a house that appeals to you, make an offer. If someone needs cash, they are not going to put this information on the sign, so you have to submit an offer to find out.

The best candidates for "fire sales" are homes owned by small builders that have been on the market for a long time. First make sure you look for the reason no one likes it. There is usually a reason. If not—and only if not—make an offer if it fits into the strategy. Keep in mind that a property is only worth what someone pays for it. If you buy a $150,000 home for $130,000, maybe it was never really worth $150,000. Make sure it's worth more than you offer. An appraisal is inexpensive insurance. Sometimes, however, a builder might think that surviving to fight another day is more important than making a profit on that particular house. Keep your eyes open for these opportunities.

20

Contracting

There are a few key elements required for a good contract:
- A good contract form
- Complete, accurate, and comprehensive contract documents (plans, specifications, allowances)
- Organization
- Thorough documentation

If you prepare thoroughly, answer all questions up front, and document the answers, you will write good contracts. Use a specification sheet like FHA Form 2005, which is available on the Web site www.hudclips.org. Go to the forms section and then to FHA forms.

Competition gives you the best results, so always get several quotes for everything. Contractors and subcontractors give you better pricing when they know that others are bidding it. Also, you inevitably get questions from one that the others forgot to ask. It gives you a better chance of getting the contract right when more than one contractor asks questions. Get three contractors to bid if you're hiring a builder, and get three subcontractors to bid any phase of work if you're building it yourself.

Use a bid sheet to track the bid information and to ensure that you compare each bidder on an "apples-to-apples" basis. Use the bid sheet similar to the one below (download it at http://books.mcgraw-hill.com/business/download/condon.) for comparing subcontractor bids. This one, which is for siding, will give you an idea of what questions to ask.

Bid Sheet Date: _____ Item: Siding	Subcontractor		
Bid Item	Ace	Omni	ABC
Siding work per plans	Yes	Yes	Yes
6-inch beaded vinyl siding 0.42 thickness	Yes	Yes	Yes
Gable vents	No	Yes	Yes
5-inch corners	Yes	Yes	Yes
Pediments	Yes	Yes	Yes
Mounting blocks for hose bibs and lights	Yes	Yes	Yes
Panel shutters	Yes	Yes	Yes
Soffit and fascia per plan	Yes	Yes	Yes
Permit or work licenses included?	Yes	Yes	Yes
Copy of their take-off?	Yes	No	No
Estimated duration	5 Days	4 Days	12 Days
Availability	Good	Good	Tied Up
References	Good	Good	Good
Insured	Yes	Yes	Yes
Bonded	Yes	Yes	Yes
Pay requirements	Weekly	Weekly	Weekly
Bid amount	$4250	$4800	$4400
Extras:			

Obviously, the specifics of the bid sheet will change with different subcontractors, but the form works for all types. There is a builder bid sheet available for download at http://books.mcgraw-hill.com/business/download/condon. It will help keep track of bids from general contractors.

Let the Fun Begin!

Once all of the bids are entered into your bid sheets, figure out who has the highest price. Call him first. Tell him, "Thanks for your bid on my house. You are not the lowest bidder. Are you sure I have your best number?" He knows he won't get the job if he says yes. He also knows he just wasted all that time bidding your house if he doesn't get the job. He may cut his price. He may even become the NEW low bidder. He will ask if that's good enough to get the job. Thank him and tell him you will review the numbers and let him know.

Now call the second highest bidder and say the same thing. "Thanks for your bid on my house. You are not the lowest bidder. Are you sure I have your best number?" Keep going until you've called them all. Do not keep going; one price cut is enough. It needs to be a fair process. They will ask you, "What number are you looking for?" or "How much high am I?" Do not answer. Tell them, "I'm not telling anyone else your number, so I won't tell you theirs. Just give me your best number." Never tell. Be fair to everyone.

Once you decide who gets the work, you can start signing them up. With subcontractors in particular, it's very tempting to take someone at their word and not write a contract. Don't do it. There are plenty of simple contracts that protect you against all the things that you hope will not go wrong.

What happens if your mason stops halfway through the job and doesn't return your calls for five weeks? It's happened. With a contract, you have a legal course of action that you both agreed to. Your contract may allow you to (1) hire someone else after 72 hours, (2) pay the replacement contractor whatever you need to, (3) pay the original contractor anything that is left, and (4) if it costs more than the contract amount to complete the work, the original contractor agrees in writing to pay you back. He WILL sign the contract up front. Who is going to tell a potential customer that he "can't sign that, because I just may leave you high and dry, and I don't want to be responsible for the damages that I cause you."

Don't misunderstand me. You can still get burned. A contract is little consolation with a subcontractor who's vanished. However, the contract gives you clear guidelines that you can use to pursue legal action if necessary. When hiring a general contractor, contracts are essential for the same reasons, the stakes are just bigger.

The Contract

The contract is a document that consists of the main "Form of Agreement" document, and the "Contract Documents" or plans, specifications, and other documents that are important in defining the project. Consulting an attorney to set up a sample contract is money well spent. They can tell you specifically how to word the language that ties all the documents together and keeps it legally binding.

Another source for a contract is the AIA, or American Institute of Architects. Contract forms are available for sale on their Web site (www.AIA.org), which has many contract documents for both commercial and residential construction. The ones that may be appropriate for you are as follows:

A101-1997, Standard Form of Agreement Between Owner and Contractor–Stipulated Sum

This is a FULL SIZE contract agreement between an Owner and a Contractor. You are the Owner. The Contractor could either be a General Contractor, if you hire one, or a Subcontractor, if you are acting as your own General Contractor. (The term "Subcontractor" is generally used to describe the working tradesman, but in this agreement it would be a "Contractor." In contract terms, a Subcontractor is one who works for the Contractor, not the Owner.) This document is very lengthy, probably more than necessary because it applies to commercial construction. With this contract, there is a guaranteed amount, or "Lump Sum," for which the Contractor agrees to perform the work. Other contract information like plans and specifications are included in the "Contract Documents" by reference.

Contracting

A201-1997, General Conditions of the Contract for Construction

This is the "General Conditions" referred to in the A101 contract document above. It must be attached to the A101 document for all contracts.

A107-1997, Abbreviated Standard Form of Agreement Between Owner and Contractor for Construction Projects of Limited Scope–Stipulated Sum

This is the abbreviated version of the Lump Sum A101 document and does not require the General Conditions A201 document. This is the document the AIA recommends for a single residential home project. Again, you are the Owner. The Contractor could either be a General Contractor, if you hire one, or a Subcontractor, if you are acting as your own General Contractor.

G701-2000, Change Order

This is a "Change Order" document. In any contract agreement, a formal change must be made to alter the original agreement terms. A Change Order is required on AIA contracts. It simply describes the change in work and the change to the contract amount. For example, to add a screen porch per attached plans and specifications, the Change Order amount is $6000. The new contract amount is $206,000.

A114-2001, Standard Form of Agreement Between Owner and Contractor (Cost Plus, no GMP)

Used with a General Contractor, this is a contract based on the cost of the work plus a fee amount (or "Cost Plus"). Instead of a fixed contract amount that the General Contractor guarantees, the General Contractor's fee is negotiated up front. The cost of the project is not guaranteed. The Owner and the Contractor keep track of the costs as they go, and the Contractor is paid a fee, which is either a percent of the contract value or a fixed fee. In this arrangement, the Contractor has no real incentive to keep costs down. In fact, a fee based on percentage of cost may even give them incentive to raise the cost of the project. If you plan a project out thoroughly, this contract is not necessary. I recommend Lump Sum or the next contract, Cost Plus GMP.

A111-1997, Standard Form of Agreement Between Owner and Contractor (Cost Plus, with a GMP)

Used with a General Contractor, this is a contract based on a "Cost Plus" amount. However, the contract also has a GMP, or "Guaranteed Maximum Price." The General Contractor's fee is negotiated up front. The cost of the project is not guaranteed unless it reaches the GMP. The Owner and the Contractor keep track of the costs as they go, and the Contractor is paid a fee, which is either a percent of the contract value or a fixed fee. If the cost of the project exceeds the GMP, the Owner pays no more than the Guaranteed Maximum Price. This allows some room for changes and flexibility and also provides a level of comfort for the Owner.

Being written by the AIA, these contract documents understandably include an architect in the process. A manual change to the forms will be required if you do not use an architect.

Choose the Right Contract!

Choosing the right contract format for a general contractor is very important because you may loose the benefit of your hard work if you do not handle the bidding process and contract forms correctly.

When asked to bid a customer's set of plans, builders often use a square footage price. Why? Generally speaking, builders can look at a plan and know about what it will cost. If they build houses for people on a regular basis with those features and specifications, they may be comfortable to give you a quote based on a price per square foot. In their belief, this will likely make them about the same amount of money as the last similar house they did. Obviously, this saves them a tremendous amount of time that might be spent on estimating and bidding. I don't like this method of bidding because it is rarely as accurate as it needs to be. However, it happens all the time. Other builders may crunch some actual numbers and give a more realistic bid.

If a builder uses a general square footage price to bid your house, the builder will reap the benefit of all of the value engineering and cost savings work that you have done! You deserve the profit. You picked the cost effective plan. You picked the cost effective materials and specifications. *That money is yours!*

Make sure builders figure out the true cost of THIS house, and add their markup to that number.

If you feel like they have scrutinized the plans and given you good bid numbers, than the Lump Sum contract is a good way to lock into a fixed cost for the project. The builder can then assume the risk of staying on budget. All you have to do at that point is monitor the quality and schedule.

If you feel that the bids from the general contractors did not reflect all of the cost savings possible, you may want to consider the Cost Plus contract with a Guaranteed Maximum Price (GMP). This contract offers *you* the ability to benefit from the cost savings ideas. ACTUAL costs are tracked as the project progresses. If the house comes in under the builder's expected costs, you save money. If costs are higher, you haven't lost anything.

Insurance

Insurance coverage is extremely important. Only use general contractors or subcontractors who have complete insurance coverage. The company that provides you with your builder's risk policy can tell you what coverage to require. Generally, I require coverage for General Liability and Workman's Compensation. General Liability Insurance protects you if his actions damage you or your property. Workman's Compensation Insurance protects the contractor's employees in the event of an injury.

Get a copy of the policy. Requiring a copy is common and absolutely necessary. Look at the coverage limits, look at the coverage DATES to ensure that the policy is in effect (and will be in effect at the time he does your work). Ask an attorney to review anything you're uncomfortable with. If a subcontractor is burning a fire to keep warm and it catches your house on fire, you want the general contractor's insurance to cover it. You want him to pay the deductible. More commonly, if a plumber's pipe leaks and ruins 1000 square feet of hardwood and all the cabinets, you want his insurance to pay for it. If the roofer falls off his ladder and injures his back, he could be out of work for six months. You don't want him on your insurance.

The limits of coverage are also important. Coverage for $1 million liability is much different than $100,000. Just having "coverage" is not good enough. Check the limits and the comments at the bottom of the certificate. Check with your insurance carrier to determine what coverage is appropriate for you.

If you act as your own general contractor, definitely get full coverage. Have it in place before doing anything, and require coverage on all subcontractors.

Subcontractor and Contractor Payments

Always remember this: The only real control you have over a subcontractor is the money. When you pay, or whether you pay, sets the stage for their next action. Pay him for work performed and NO MORE. His finances have nothing to do with you. You need to remember this point. If he goes away, you have to pay someone else to finish it. That is ALWAYS more expensive because no one likes to complete someone else's work. Hold enough money back to get the job done by someone else.

I have learned this the hard way MANY times. It's hard not to pay someone in that situation. The only way to prevent it is to tell him up front that you will not let him get ahead of you on the money, and remind him when he asks you. Also, have the discussion by your car, for a quick getaway.

Much like subcontractor payments, pay the general contractor ONLY for work completed. Your lender will have a protocol for paying your general contractor. Never pay too much money early in the process.

Lien Waivers

There are laws providing subcontractors and suppliers with protection against nonpayment. Liens can be applied against your home if a contractor or subcontractor did not pay for the material or labor used in your house.

For example: You pay a mason to perform the brickwork (labor and material). You pay him upon completion. He fails to pay for the bricks. The brick supplier has legal rights to come after you! If the supplier files a mechanic's lien, you would need to pay him for the bricks before the lien would be removed. Closing cannot occur with a lien on the property.

Yes, it stinks for you, but it can happen. Lien waivers are documents that have the contractor or subcontractor state that all bills are paid and they will not allow a lien to go against your home. Contractors should sign a lien waiver before receiving each check from you.

Consult an attorney to find out about liens in your state.

Attorneys

I know that this isn't the first time I said to consult an attorney, but laws vary from state to state. These issues can be very serious if you end up on the wrong end of a bad situation. With major investments like homes, take no chances. Make a long list of questions to ask an attorney, make an appointment, and talk really fast.

Volume Is King

If you're planning to build several rental properties, lumping them together in a single contract agreement will give you buying power with either a general contractor or subcontractors. You can have each house on a separate contract but bid them as a group to drive home the point that there is a good bit of work here. This means a lot in terms of the price you receive.

Contracting on one plan that can be built repeatedly is an effective approach as well. One or two great plans can be built many times in the same community as long as they are sufficiently separated. Even building the same house in different parts of town is beneficial to you, as well as the subcontractors and the contractor. It's one less estimate they need to produce. Just make sure they pass that efficiency on to you.

21

Financing

Saving the most important for last, how do you pay for this? There are many ways and we will not get into the fine details of all of them. There are a few common methods. I suggest first speaking with your bank. Many full-service banks can provide complete financing. Since they know your account history and vital information, it takes a step out of the process. I can't tell you everything about loans, mortgages, and other potential resources. Lending institutions will tell you about their current programs when you visit them. However, I will try to tell you some things that they won't.

Construction/Permanent Loan

This is how I financed all four of my personal houses. A "construction/perm," as they call it, is a loan package that is actually two loans in one. The first part of the loan is set up to facilitate home construction and its specific loan needs. Upon completion of the house, the loan can be converted into a typical permanent loan. There is a "closing" before any money is loaned. At that point you basically open a line of credit. You ask for permission to borrow up to a certain amount. That maximum amount is the "loan amount." You close on the loan, and you may even take your first draw at that time.

A "draw" is a borrowed amount that is given to you in the form of a single check or wire transfer into your account. You may want to take a draw at closing to pay for the lot. You take draws as needed throughout construction in order to pay for work and materials. There are many restrictions on when you can take draws and how much money you can borrow. We'll get into that later in this chapter. When you near completion on the home, you take your final draw for the amount you need to pay the rest of the bills. At that point you may have borrowed $200,000 against a loan amount of $220,000. If you don't need the other money, that's fine. You can convert the ultimate loan amount— $200,000 in this case—to a permanent loan. The conversion usually involves a few forms and not a full closing. This is important because closings cost money.

Construction Loan

A construction loan is typically an interest only loan. Unlike most other loans, the principal is not paid monthly along with interest. You take a draw, and use the money to buy materials and labor. At the end of the month you get an invoice for the interest on the outstanding balance. The interest payment goes up each month as you borrow more money. The interest bills can be paid with some of the money you borrowed. Interest payments do not need to come out of your pocket.

Money-saving techniques you can use:

- **Do not overestimate the loan amount.** You will note that in the previous example, the loan was $220,000 and only $200,000 was used. This can waste money. When you close on a construction/perm, you pay "points" on the loan. A point is 1 percent of the loan value. So if you pay 2 points as an "origination fee," you're paying 2 percent of the loan value; 2 percent of $220,000 is $4400. This is, effectively, interest that the bank gets up front. If your loan value is way too high, you're paying points on money that you will never borrow. For example, 2 percent of $20,000 is $400. You sure don't want to run out of money, but don't be overly conservative either. Have a good idea what the house will cost before you close on the loan.

- **Draw the right amount.** Before a draw is approved for payment, a bank inspector may look at your home to see if a draw, or fund disbursement, is justified. Most construction loans allow a certain number of inspections before they start charging you. This forces you to budget your money well, know what expenses are coming due, and allow time to get a draw check into your account in time to pay people. If you're allowed five draws free and then you are charged $75 per inspection, you need to decide which is more expensive, the interest or the inspection fee. If you have a lot of money borrowed, the interest you save by taking smaller and more frequent draws may more than cover a few inspection fees. The natural reaction would be to borrow money in big chunks. For me, that meant having a large balance in a non-interest-bearing account for a long time until I ran out. I would have paid interest on the loan that whole time and lost money in the end. I ended up taking smaller and more frequent draws. If your fees are higher or your interest lower, your decision may be different.

Different lending institutions have different rules associated with their loans. Pay very close attention to when a draw is allowed. Some lenders require the house to be dried-in before the first draw can be made against *the house*. "Dried-in" means that the framing is complete, the roof is on, and windows/doors are installed. The lender may want the house protected from weather in case you cannot finish it. Unless it is protected, extensive weather damage could occur before they were able to take over construction and finish it in the case of your default on the loan. Getting to dry-in takes a lot of money and can be a huge cash flow issue. There are four ways to approach this hurdle:

1. Have enough cash to buy the lot and build the house to the dry-in stage. This is obviously tough.

2. Pay for the lot with cash and take a lot draw at loan closing. If you own the land outright, lenders will lend you money against the lot before construction begins, because if you default, they can sell the lot to recoup their investment. So you take a lot draw for most of the value of the lot and use the money to pay for construction of the house to the dry-in stage. Two tricks with this approach are to have funds to buy the lot and to delay as many bills as possible until your second draw. If you negotiate your terms with the lumber supplier and build fast, most of your costs will be framing labor and foundation. Bills for your windows, doors, and shingles will come in well after your second draw is in the bank.

3. A home equity loan may be an option if you have equity in the house that you currently live in (and have not yet sold). Equity in rental properties works just as well. A home equity loan gives you the cash you need to finance the new construction on your new house. You pay off the home equity loan when you sell your house (the old one).

4. You can use equity from a house you just sold. Circumstances caused me to sell the first three houses before I started construction on my next one. We moved into an apartment in the interim. We had our profit (equity) in the bank. We used this money to buy the next lot. It usually paid for some construction as well, before running out. I used savings or other short-term investment money to tide me over for the few extra weeks it took to get to dry-in.

The fourth approach obviously only works if you sell your house first, though that was not quite so obvious to me on my last house. I wanted to build a new one while still living in my previous house, and I was so used to funding not being a problem that I forgot to think it through. I was ready to close on my lot when I realized that I didn't have the big fat checking account with my equity sitting in it. After a brief panic, the third technique, above, occurred to me—to get a home equity loan on the house I was living in. I used that second mortgage on my house to cover lot and dry-in costs. Of course, the easiest way around this whole issue is to get a loan that does not require the home to be dried-in before the first draw against the house.

Another important aspect of many construction loans is that the lender only pays you a percentage of the completed work. For example: You may apply for a draw and have $100,000 worth of work in place. The lender may agree that $100,000 worth of work is done. They may still only pay you 90 percent, or $90,000. This means that it's up to you to make up the difference. This is an important cash flow consideration. The percentage may vary. Ask your lender.

Permanent Mortgage

There are many types of permanent loans available. Not all options may be available with a construction/perm, so ask the right questions. They are all repaid monthly over a given time period. Monthly payments include both principle and interest. The most common types of permanent loans are:

Conventional. A conventional loan is any permanent, long-term financing that is not V.A. or FHA.

V.A. The Veterans Administration provides a loan program that gives veterans access to a loan with easy qualifications and no down payment. V.A. guarantees the loan. A funding fee is paid up front, but it can be rolled into the loan amount.

FHA. The Federal Housing Administration provides lenders with an insurance policy that eliminates the lender's risk. There are limitations on FHA loans, and the borrower pays an initial premium for the insurance (MIP) as well as a monthly premium.

The type of a permanent mortgage vary with the lender, but most lenders offer the following:

Fixed rate mortgage. Over the life of the amortized loan, the rate of interest is constant. The typical amortized term may be 30, 25, 20, or 15 years. Other terms are available.

Adjustable rate mortgage (ARM). There are many variations of this type of permanent long-term flexible loan, but in all cases the interest rate rises or falls according to some external index (e.g., the prime index). Some forms of this mortgage have a period of time at the beginning that has a fixed interest rate. A 3/1 ARM is an adjustable rate mortgage that has a fixed rate for the first three years and an adjustable rate for the remainder of the mortgage.

There are several other types of mortgages, but these are the ones you'll likely end up with after consulting your lender. Fixed rates are the most stable. It will be the same payment for the life of the loan. An ARM is a great deal in the short term. If you plan to sell the house within the fixed introductory period of a 3/1 or 5/1 ARM, you can really save on interest. Things can change, though. You may need to stay in that house for longer than you thought, so make sure that you can live with the interest rate when it climbs.

Home Equity Loan

If the amount of equity in your home is higher than the amount of the mortgage, you can use a home equity loan as your primary mortgage. There are other benefits to a home equity loan. When you close on the loan, you can basically get the option to borrow up to a certain amount of money. You can make that number as high as you want, or as high as your equity amount will allow. This essentially creates an open line of credit. Other purchases can be made with this line of credit. Autos, boats, and purchases that may involve interest loans will now have tax deductible interest. Personally, my goal was to eliminate mortgage payments; running up debt on home equity goes against my plan. But you can still have the credit should you find yourself in need someday.

Loan Terms That Can Cost Money

Origination Fee

Origination fees are fees charged by a lender to create the loan. You can basically consider this interest charged up front. Lenders compete for your business and try to get your attention with a low interest rate. An attractive rate may be accompanied by a high origination fee. A loan with a low origination fee, or none at all, may have a higher interest rate. When shopping for a loan, it is often hard to determine the true cost of each. Try. They are in the business to make money. They get paid one way or another.

Financing

Discount Points

In order to get a lower interest rate, you may pay discount points to "buy down" the interest rate. Again, lenders get paid one way or another. Discount points are also essentially interest payments paid up front. Since a point is 1 percent of the loan value, you may pay 2 points to buy down your interest rate. You will then have a lower monthly payment since the interest is lower. Depending on costs, it may pay for itself over a long period of time. This may not be a worthwhile investment if you plan to move anytime soon. Typically, you will pay more in total costs if you move in a few years.

Settlement Statement

A real estate closing or a loan closing can be a very confusing event. There are seemingly hundreds of documents to sign. You can't possibly read everything while you're sitting there, but you are expected to sign documents saying that you understand what you have read. The attorney's job is to guide you through it and make sure all of the numbers add up, the documents are correct, and documents get processed correctly after the closing.

My wife used to scrutinize settlement statements and ask all of the time-consuming questions that slow up the closing. I would feel uneasy and sometimes annoyed about it until the attorney would say, "Yes, ma'am, you're right. That figure is incorrect." It has happened several times and always would have cost us hundreds of dollars. I no longer consider her questions annoying.

There is often a lot of confusing math and confusing conditions in a real estate transaction. You are not the only one that gets confused. The attorneys typically have people prepare the documents. If they misunderstand some part of the transaction, they can give the wrong information to the attorney when he checks everything. This is what happened to us several times. Asking questions about anything on the settlement statement that does not make perfect sense will sometimes expose that innocent mistake. The moral: Do not be afraid to ask about anything.

Loan Lock

Interest rates go up and down all the time. You may get a quote for an interest rate one day, and the next day the rate is different. In times of change, rates can change substantially from morning to afternoon as the lender gets notice of rate changes. More often, rates are consistent over longer periods of time.

At some point in time you commit to a certain interest rate, and the lender commits that rate to you. The farther away from closing, the more risk the lender has. Therefore, the farther away you are from closing on a property, the more expensive it is to lock the interest rate. A "30-day lock" allows you to lock into an interest rate for 30 days. It means that you must close within 30 days of your lock date. A "90-day lock" costs more money because it's farther away from closing.

The problem with locks is that you're gambling that you will be ABLE to close within that time period. I have seen many people lock into a rate and not be able to close within the time period. This can cost a lot of money, depending on what interest rates are doing. Ask MANY questions about the requirements of such locks. What happens if they expire? Can they be extended? How much will that cost? But the most important question of all is: "When will the house be done?" Answer that with confidence, and add some time for the unexpected. If rates are increasing, this can be expensive to miscalculate.

MIP/PMI

MIP stands for "mortgage insurance premiums" (FHA loans). PMI stands for "private mortgage insurance" (conventional loans).

Depending on your loan type, you may pay one of these two types of mortgage insurance. If you have more than 20 percent equity in your home, PMI is not required on a conventional loan. An 80 percent "loan to value ratio," or LTV, is an 80 percent loan. This leaves 20 percent equity. If you have less than 20 percent equity, the monthly insurance payment is required. For example: A house worth $100,000 that has a mortgage of $82,000 has an LTV of 82 percent. This is more than 80 percent, so PMI is required. On an FHA loan, the threshold is a loan to value ratio of 78 percent. As soon as you exceed 22 percent equity, you can stop paying MIP and start saving money.

Look Competent

When you start to talk with lenders, have your ducks in a row and look competent. You do not want to appear like a risk to them. If you have no building experience and no clue, you are a big risk. In order to get their money back, they may have to jump in to clean up your mess if you fail. You want to look well-researched and confident. You need to demonstrate some of the knowledge you have taken away from this book. You need to know what and where you intend to build, and how much you need to borrow. With the Internet, you can do a lot of homework on lending before you show up in person. Start your face-to-face conversations with your bank to see what they have to offer.

If you find yourself unable to get construction financing because you do not have a licensed general contractor, there's a solution: Become licensed yourself. As we discussed, sometimes this makes sense.

One final thought: There is no shortage of people out there who are licensed with only enough building knowledge to pass the test. This is why there is no substitute for references and a proven track record of success.

22

The Moment of Truth

The time has come to decide how you should build your house. If you think you can do it, act as your own general contractor. You'll have a great experience. I guarantee you will never forget it.

If you plan to hire a manager or a general contractor, buy them a copy of this book so they will approach the construction of your home with the same approach as you. They need to understand your motives. I can assure you, you won't be approaching the construction process like the rest of their customers. Ask the general contractor or manager to look for things in this book that might be different in your market. Get it all straight up front. If they claim that something will not work in your area, or that the cost savings ideas are too strange, challenge them.

I have hired more than a few ex-builders over the years who had their own companies and lost them. Occasionally they will challenge something we do by saying, "I never did that. I built houses for years without ever doing that." I've never had the nerve to say what I was thinking, and that is: "If you did do it the right way, you might still be in business for yourself instead of working here!" Anyway, resolve any differences or points of contention, and agree on how the project will proceed.

Knowledge and discipline equal profits. If you apply the knowledge you've learned from this book AND have the discipline to stick to only what is profitable, your home-building experience will be rewarding.

For me, I love the feeling of accomplishment at the end of a productive day. I like seeing what work got done as I drive up after work. I like the fact that my wife has the same goals and agrees that the sacrifices in time and energy are worth it (this is critical for success). I also love when some days were finally over. No matter how good a job you do, there will be a few days that you'd rather forget. Forget them and keep plugging away. The payoff is big. The reward is there for the taking. With the new capital gains laws, it's even bigger. Keep the end in mind and everything else in perspective. Good luck!

Some Assembly Required is a companion book to *Building Real Estate Riches* that provides all the trade secrets to effectively manage the home-building process. From estimating, budgeting, and scheduling to a comprehensive quality control program, this book is the instruction manual for home building. Look for the link at http://books.mcgraw-hill.com/business/download/condon to learn more and order a copy.

Glossary of Terms

Amenities Facilities or features of a community that are created for common use by the residents of the community; for example, pool, tennis courts, soccer fields, jogging trails, etc.

Appraiser Professional who estimates the market price of real estate.

Arborist Professional who specializes in tree protection.

Attic The unfinished area above the ceiling and below the roof.

Backfill Dirt or soil that is placed into a cavity and compacted. Cavities may include garages, porches, etc.

Balusters Vertical trim pieces, pickets, or spindles supporting a handrail.

Basement A foundation that is belowground and is habitable. It may be finished or unfinished, but will at least have a permanent floor.

Glossary of Terms

Box ceiling   A rectangular cavity that is recessed into a room's ceiling for decorative purposes. The surfaces of a box ceiling are all at right angles to each other.

Builder   The company or person responsible for the construction of the home (see *General contractor*).

Building paper (or **felt paper** or **tar paper**)   Tar-impregnated paper installed over the roof sheathing as an additional layer of protection under the shingles. Building paper can also be used over wall sheathing as a moisture barrier for siding or masonry.

Cantilever   A projecting beam or floor structure that overhangs the wall or supporting member below.

Chimney   The vertical shaft of a fireplace used for removing the smoke from the fire.

Community Covenants and Restrictions (CC&Rs)   A legal document tied to the deed of a property in a community that requires the land owner to comply with the restrictions of the community. Restrictions generally dictate architectural guidelines as well as permitted uses for the property.

Common areas   Areas of land in a community that the developer permanently dedicates for use and enjoyment of the residents of that community.

Compacted soil   Soil placed in layers of approximately 12 inches and tamped in place to eliminate air voids in the soil. Properly compacted soil reaches a density that will support the weight of construction.

Cornice   A decorative horizontal element projecting near the top of the wall.

Crawl space   A foundation type that uses masonry or concrete walls and piers to raise the first floor of a house off the ground. The interior of a crawl space is not a finished space and is often exposed ground with a thin layer of plastic film (poly).

Developer   The term refers to the company that created the community and installed the infrastructure, including the sewer, water, curbs, paving, streetlights, etc. The developer is often the entity selling the lots.

Glossary of Terms

Dormer   A projection in a sloping roof that encloses a window, which is set upright.

Down spout   The pipe that takes the water down from the gutters and discharges it away from the house.

Drop sill   The beam supporting the floor joists in a crawl space.

Drywall   Also called **Sheetrock** or **gypsum wallboard (GWB)**, drywall is a gypsum-based wall covering material. Wall boards are typically 4 feet by 12 feet by ½ inches, and ceiling boards are typically 4 feet by 12 feet by ⅝ inches.

Elevation   The view of a house, or a portion thereof, that shows height or vertical surfaces. Elevations are typically drawings of the exterior of a house.

Expansive soil   Soils that expand excessively when moist and shrink when dry. These soils swell and create extensive damage to foundations.

Fascia   The vertical board at the edge of a roof just below the shingles and just above the soffit.

Felt paper   See *Building paper.*

Finger joint   Interior trim and some other lumber use this type of joint to splice small pieces of wood together to create very long, straight, and stable lumber that is paint grade (not for staining). The strong joints resemble interwoven fingers.

Finish grade   The top of the ground on the building site, but often refers to the top of the ground right at the edge of the house.

Finished basement   A basement that has complete interior finishes, including wall and floor coverings and conditioned air.

Flood plain   An area susceptible to flood damage from high water from rain or bodies of water. Often labeled in terms of time, a 100-year flood plain would be an area that would be affected by waters from a flood as bad as any in the last 100 years. A 100-year flood would have higher flood waters than a 50-year flood. The higher the number of years, the more severe the flood.

Floor plan   A drawing that shows the horizontal layout of a house, or portion thereof. The term is often used to describe the main house layout.

Footing The concrete pad that carries the weight of the house and transfers it to the ground.

Footprint The outside perimeter of a house.

Foundation The structure that supports the house, typically made of concrete or masonry.

French drain A perforated plastic pipe buried in a bed of stone belowground that aids water drainage.

Gable The triangular end of a building's roof.

Gable vent A louver in the top of the gable to allow for attic ventilation.

General contractor (GC) The company responsible for the construction of the home. The GC hires material suppliers and subcontractors directly to perform work under the primary contract with the owner of the home. The GC is ultimately responsible for all actions and work performed by subcontractors.

Geotechnical firm A company that analyzes soils and provides technical services to determine if soil is of suitable composition and is properly compacted.

GFCI The **Ground Fault Circuit Interrupt** (sometimes called GFI) is a special electrical circuit with special outlets (plugs) that protect people from electrical shock through the use of a circuit breaker located on the outlet.

Gutter The metal trough that gathers rainwater from the roof.

Habitable space Space in a house that is inhabited, or regular living space complying with all applicable codes.

Header A beam over a door opening, window opening, or another type of opening.

Hearth The floor of the fireplace that extends into the room to protect the floor from burning embers.

Hip roof A roof that slopes inward on all (four) sides instead of having a gable end.

Hollow core doors   Doors made with a thin veneer of material over a frame. The interior cavity may be hollow or insulated.

Home Owner's Association (HOA)   A group of property owners who manage the affairs of the community, including budgetary expenses and rule enforcement.

HVAC   Stands for heating, ventilation, and air-conditioning. The system that heats and cools the home.

I-joist   A manufactured joist with a cross section that resembles the letter I.

Impact fee   A fee imposed by a local jurisdiction on new construction.

Insulation   A material used to keep a home warm in the winter and cool in the summer. It's placed in the walls, attic, and any surface adjacent to the exterior of a home.

Jack   A stud in a wall opening that supports a header; also known as a "trimmer stud."

Joist   The structural members or beams that hold up the floor or ceiling.

Lintel   The structural member used over windows, doors, or other openings to support masonry.

Lot premium   An additional cost associated with the purchase of a parcel of land (lot) due to the increased appeal/value of that particular lot.

Mono (monolithic) slabs   A concrete foundation slab poured in a single pour (monolithically) with the footing concrete. The footing, slab edges, and slab are all one single structure. As a result, mono slabs are generally very low to the ground.

Newel   The post that terminates a length of railing.

One-story   A home with all rooms on a single level.

One-and-a-half-story   A home with most rooms on a lower main level and a few rooms in a small, less conspicuous upstairs.

Organic soil (organic matter)   Soil with roots, leaves, grass, plants, or other material that has not yet fully decomposed. As matter decomposes, it shrinks. This can cause problems to a home by causing the house to move and settle over time as the organic soil decomposes.

OSB (Oriented Strand Board)   A sheathing material made of small strips of wood glued and pressed together. Highly strong and environmentally friendly, OSB is commonly used as roof, wall, and floor sheathing.

Pediments   Decorative features mounted above a window on the exterior of a house.

Perk   Ground is said to perk when a fixed amount of water can soak into the ground in a fixed amount of time. The ability of ground to perk allows it to support a septic tank. Soil absorption is necessary to allow the septic tank waste to dissipate into the soil through a septic field.

Perk test   A hole of exact size is dug in the ground in the desired location of a septic field. The hole is filled with an exact quantity of water. If the hole is empty in a certain amount of time, the land "perks."

Plan drawing   A drawing that shows the horizontal layout of a house, or portion thereof. The term "floor plan" is often used to describe the main house layout.

Plate   The board located at the top and bottom of the wall studs.

Plot plan   A plan created by a surveyor that shows the orientation of the house on the homesite. All critical dimensions are shown: building setbacks, easements, and lot dimensions.

Pony wall   A wood-framed foundation wall with siding used in crawl space foundations. The pony wall is used in lieu of the more expensive material, like masonry or concrete, used in the remainder of the foundation.

Ridge   The top intersection of two opposite adjoining roof surfaces.

Ridge vent   Metal or plastic caps nailed to the ridge of a roof used to ventilate the attic.

Glossary of Terms

Riser   The vertical portion of a set of steps that connects the horizontal tread surfaces.

Roof pitch   Describes the severity of the slope of a roof. Roof pitch is referred to as a comparison of rise to run, or vertical height to horizontal length in a given measurement. For example: 7 feet of height (rise) in a 12-foot horizontal distance (run) is a 7/12 roof pitch.

Roof rafters   The structural members that support the roof if it is built with conventional (or stick-built) framing.

Septic field   The distribution mechanism for a septic system. Perforated pipes embedded in gravel stretch out underground, allowing the liquid waste to dissipate into the soil.

Septic tank   The reservoir tank in a septic system. The waste is contained and treated in the tank before being dissipated into the soil through the septic field.

Sewer line (sewer lateral)   A pipe that connects the public sewer pipe to the house sewer discharge.

Sewer tap   The connection between the builder's sewer line to the house and the public sewer. Taps are typically installed by the developer and the location is marked. When the builder installs the sewer line to the house, the tap is exposed and the connection is made.

Sewer tap fee   The fee charged by the local municipality to allow a builder to tie into the sewer system. The fee is charged to offset the expense of installing the system.

Sheathing   The thin layer on the covering over the roof, wall, and floor structural members. Sheathing is usually four by eight feet. Floor and roof sheathing is structural, while wall sheathing may or may not be structural.

Side light   A narrow window unit flanking a door. Side lights are often integral with the door unit.

Sill   The board affixed to the foundation and on which the floor or wall members rest.

Glossary of Terms

Single hung window A window whose lower sash is operable and whose upper sash is fixed in place.

Skylights A window unit installed in the roof and following the slope of the roof. It can be fixed or operable.

Slab The layer of concrete that is the structural floor. Slabs can be inside the house or in the garage. Outside concrete structures such as a driveway or patio are sometimes referred to as "concrete slabs."

Slab foundation A type of foundation that includes a concrete slab as the floor surface. A slab foundation may be low to the ground or raised up off the ground. The raised slabs (or stemwall slabs) are often made of a perimeter wall, interior fill dirt, and a concrete slab. The perimeter walls are commonly masonry or concrete.

Slope The rising or falling of ground; an incline; a slant.

Soffit The flat horizontal surface under the end of a roof, just below the fascia; sometimes referred to as an "eave."

Span The length of a beam or joist in between supports.

Stair stringer The sloping board that supports the ends of each tread and riser.

Studs The vertical wood members in a wall, usually two by four inches and spaced 16 inches on center.

Subflooring Sheathing laid over the floor joists.

Swail (drainage swail) A shallow ditch or depression in the yard used to divert water around and away from the house.

Tar paper See *Building paper.*

Termite treatment A chemical pesticide treatment to protect a house from infestation by termites.

Title Ownership of real estate. A marketable title is one that has no defects, liens, legal rights, or claims against it and has clear ownership.

Tongue and groove A method of connection between pieces of lumber that uses a thin protrusion (tongue) from one board to lock into a groove in another board. This connection prevents vertical displacement.

Transom A small horizontal strip of glass above a door or cased opening.

Tray ceiling A rectangular cavity recessed into a room's ceiling for decorative purposes. The vertical surfaces of the tray are angled in slightly as it projects into the ceiling.

Tread The horizontal board in a set of stairs that is stepped on when stairs are used.

Tree save areas Areas that have been preserved from clearing to protect the trees. Some trees may be protected because of their size without being inside an identified area.

Trusses Preengineered structural components that utilize smaller sizes of lumber to create a structural unit of superior strength. Roof trusses support the roof while providing a ceiling for the rooms below. Floor trusses can be used in lieu of traditional lumber joists to allow larger spans and create room for mechanical piping.

Two-story A house that has rooms on two levels.

Unfinished basement A basement that has only enough work completed to provide the structure of the house and minimum code requirements such as basic lighting and access. No finish materials are installed. The rough material of the foundation is left exposed forever or the basement can be finished at a later date.

Vapor barrier A thin layer of material used to stop water vapor from traveling through a wall or floor.

Vaulted ceiling A ceiling that slopes upward.

Vendor A material supplier that does not perform actual work on the job site.

Vinyl siding A siding made of vinyl that provides a durable low-maintenance finish.

Glossary of Terms

Walk-out basement A basement foundation that has one or more sides buried and one or more sides aboveground. Walk-out basements are installed on sloping lots and allow windows and doors to be installed in the exposed basement walls.

Water line (water lateral) A pipe that connects the public water system to the water supply pipe at the house.

Water tap The connection between the builder's water line to the house and the public water. Taps are typically installed by the developer. The location is either marked for future connection or the water meter is installed.

Water tap fee The fee charged by the local municipality to allow a builder to tie into the water system. The fee is charged to offset the expense of installing the system.

Web floor trusses Preengineered structural components that utilize smaller sizes of lumber to create a structural unit of superior strength. Web floor trusses can be used in lieu of traditional lumber joists to allow larger spans. The space between the cross members (webs) creates room for mechanical piping and ductwork.

Well A deep hole in the ground with a pump used to extract water from the ground on a lot that does not have access to a municipal water system. Wells are drilled down to varying depths until water is found.

Wetlands Areas that have standing water (at least sometimes). Wetlands have important microbiological life that is often protected by law. Some jurisdictions place a buffer around wetlands to prevent construction activities.

Window well A structure that creates a cavity around a window or door that is below ground level. Wells are often made of plastic, masonry, or metal. They are used to allow light and access to a basement space that might otherwise only have very small windows at ceiling height.

Zoning Land regulations dictating the type and use of buildings allowed on the land. Local jurisdictions create different zoning classifications for each type building: single family, multifamily, commercial, etc.

Index

Locators in **bold** indicate glossary definitions.

Index

Index

Index

Index

Index

Index

One-and-a-half-story house, 33, **163**
One-story house, 33, **163**
Open floor plans, 75–76
"Openness" in house plans, 76
Organic (decomposing) soils, 19, **163–164**
Oriented Strand Board (OSB), 104, **164**
Origination fee, 152
OSB (Oriented Strand Board), 104, **164**
Overbuilding, and investment return, 54–55, 59–60

Painting, 118, 123–125
Panelize vs. stick-building, framing, 96
Pediments, **164**
Perk, 18, 20, **164**
Perk test, 18, 20, **164**
Permanent mortgage loan, 151–152
Plan drawing, **164**
Plate, **164**
Plot plan, **164**
Plumbing, 105–106
PMI (private mortgage insurance), 154
Points, financing, 153
Pony wall, 32, **164**
Porch, 94, 97, 114
Post tension foundations, 29
Prairie architectural style, 36
Premium lots, 12
Primary residence and Equity Strategy, 4–7
Property management, 129
Property Management for Dummies (Griswold), 130

Raised slab foundations, 29
Redlines on house plans, 50
Rental properties, 127–130
    books on, 130
    cash flow strategy, 3–4, 129
    Limited Liability Corporation (LLC), 130
    property management, 129
    renters, 128
Residential lot (*see* Lot considerations and selection)

Resources and books, 130, 133
Restricted communities, 12
Ridge, **164**
Ridge vent, **164**
Riser, **165**
Rock on lot, 19
Roof and eaves, 85, 86–88, 98, 100–102, 103, 104, 109
Roof pitch, **165**
Roof rafters, **165**
Rooms:
    bedrooms, master, importance of, 79–80
    family room, importance of, 81
    house plan needs determination, 47
    size and cost saving, 86, 92–93
    time spent in, 79–81
    (*See also* Bathrooms; Kitchens)
Row houses, 34

Sales comparison approach to appraisal, 57–60
Schools and lot location, 10
Screens, window, 122
Second mortgage, 150
Septic field, **165**
Septic system, 18, 20
Septic tank, **165**
Setback lines, 20
Settlement statement, 153
Sewer line (sewer lateral), **165**
Sewer tap, **165**
Sewer tap fee, 20, **165**
Shape of lot, 19–20
Sheathing, 104–105, **165**
"Shopping" the market, 64–67
    new home builders and communities, 64–65
    notes and checklist, 65–67
Side light, **165**
Sill, **165**
Single hung window, **166**
Size:
    of house, 39–41
    of lot, 19–20
    of rooms, 86, 92–93
Skylights, **166**
Slab, **166**

Index

Index

About the Author

Christopher Condon is vice president of a market-leading home builder that builds 350 homes per year. He has worked for two of the nation's largest top 10 home builders. Over his career, Chris has managed the construction of everything from hospitals, office buildings, shopping centers, and renovation projects to new homes. As well as being a licensed home builder, Chris is licensed to sell real estate and is a patent pending inventor. He graduated with a degree in Building Science from the College of Architecture at Clemson University.

Chris has spent most of the last decade finding the best ways to profitably design and build houses and has a unique perspective on building a home that can make you money.

9 780071 436830